HALL OF FAITH SERIES

Mission in the Clouds

The Story of Orley and Lillian Ford

EILEEN E. LANTRY

Pacific Press Publishing Association
Boise, Idaho
Oshawa, Ontario, Canada

Edited by Glen Robinson
Designed by Consuelo Udave
Cover by Jim Padgett
Type set in 10/12 Century Schoolbook

Copyright © 1990 by
Pacific Press Publishing Association
Printed in United States of America
All Rights Reserved

Library of Congress Catalog Card Number: 89-62154

ISBN 0-8163-0871-3

90 91 92 93 94 • 5 4 3 2 1

Contents

Chapter	1:	Something Better	5
Chapter	2:	Enemy Attacks	9
Chapter	3:	The Call to Ecuador	14
Chapter	4:	Mission Miracles	19
Chapter	5:	Challenge at Colta Mission	23
Chapter	6:	Turmoil, Trust, Peace	28
Chapter	7:	Adventures Galore!	35
Chapter	8:	Guatemala for God	42
Chapter	9:	Their Ultimate Sacrifice	48
Chapter	10:	Living on Promise	54
Chapter	11:	Challenges Never Cease	61
Chapter	12:	The Greatest of These	66
Chapter	13:	Servants of the Lord	74

Dedication

To the Fords' two children, Elden Ford and Sylvia Larson, who have followed their parents in lives of service for God and whose input has contributed much to the preparation of this book.

Chapter 1
Something Better

A heartbroken young couple lingered near the baggage car, watching silently as the train's porter lifted a small trunk from his cart and shoved it through the open door. But when he tossed several heavy bags on top of the trunk, the young woman gasped out a desperate, "Oh, no!"

Putting his arm around her shoulders, her husband choked a sob. He then gently led her away, whispering, "Come, Lillian; let's find our seats in the passenger car and wait there."

For several minutes they sat quietly, holding hands, tears rolling down their cheeks. Finally, Lillian voiced the question uppermost in their minds.

"Why, Orley? Why didn't God heal our little Teddy?" Just a few weeks earlier, they had left their mission home in Pomata with a happy, healthy baby boy, filled with excitement over the prospect of a few weeks of rest and recuperation away from the cold and high altitudes of the Andes Mountains.

"And now, we're going home with our precious baby wrapped in his blue blanket," she sobbed, "lying alone in the trunk in that awful baggage car."

"Shhh, Lillian, someone might hear you," Orley said. "If the railroad authorities knew a dead baby was wrapped in that trunk, they wouldn't allow us to take him to Puno. And it's so important that we have him near us in our little cemetery at Plateria Mission."

"At least he'll rest beside the other children of missionary parents who wait for Jesus to awaken them," Lillian said.

6 MISSION IN THE CLOUDS

"Just think how Teddy will laugh with glee when the angel carries him swiftly through the air to us again," said Orley.

"My arms just ache to hold him close." Lillian began to cry again.

Just then they heard the whistle of the engine and felt the first lurch as the train began to move. Soon, they left the beautiful city of Arequipa, Peru, located 7,500 feet up the steep ascent of the Andes Mountains. Traveling on the world's highest standard gauge railway, Orley and Lillian Ford would literally reach the "roof of the world" in just eight hours.

Though their eyes stared out the train window, neither Lillian nor Orley noticed the magnificent scenery. They seemed unaware of the awesome precipices on one side of the train and the wall of icy peaks on the other side. They had lived on the high plateau surrounding Lake Titicaca for several years. Still they, like the other passengers, found it hard to breathe as the air became thinner. Some got mountain sickness and had to receive oxygen from tanks the train always carried.

As the train slowly chugged upward from one switchback to another, Lillian talked about her baby again.

"If only the doctors could have stopped the infection that spread so rapidly, or reduced his high fever! Little Teddy seemed so healthy and strong. Remember how well he stood that awful sixty-mile trip just a short time ago from Pomata Mission to the meeting at Plateria Mission?"

"Yes," Orley said, smiling faintly. "He looked so cute tucked in a basket on one side of a mule, with a balancing basket of baggage on the other side. He even slept through that terrible rainstorm. I'm sure God saved your life when your horse was startled by that lightning and thunder and ran away."

"That was a terrifying ride! I leaned forward and hugged his neck as he leaped over ditches and stone walls. You'd buttoned my raincoat up so well, and tucked the bottom of the long coat into the stirrups, I feared the horse might drag me along. But when he bucked, the raincoat opened up so I could fall off. I still have some black-and-blue spots from landing on that stone pile."

"Was I ever glad when I heard your horse's loud neigh,"

Orley added. "Otherwise, you might have lain there in the darkness a long while. Later we found Teddy, safe in the arms of the Indian who led the mules. I was so thankful his mule didn't become startled and run away too."

Slowly the train chugged into Puno, located on the banks of icy Lake Titicaca, 12,507 feet above sea level. This highest navigable lake in the world lay on the border of Peru and Bolivia. Surrounding it were hundreds of villages where Indians drank alcohol or chewed coca leaves, from which cocaine is produced, to forget their ever-present enemies—hunger and cold. Living mostly on barley and walnut-size frozen potatoes, they were enslaved by the rich Peruvian landowners. "How will we travel from Puno to Plateria?" Lillian asked.

"I'll rent some horses, and we'll ride along the lakeshore. We dare not take Teddy on one of the lake steamers. I'm sure I can hire some carriers to take the baby."

"But it's over eighty miles on the old Inca highway," she said. "And it's so cold by horseback!"

"I know, dear, but there's no other way. Let's trust Jesus to comfort and sustain us."

Once they had secured the precious little trunk, Lillian stayed with it until Orley had found both horses and carriers. Carefully wrapping the precious little body, they then suspended it from a pole carried by two Indians.

After resting at Plateria Mission, they continued on the sixty miles to Pomata Mission. Each group of Indians they met asked, "Where is Iscabilacajucha?" The Indians had loved the little white baby and affectionately called him, "Iscabilacajucha," which meant "Little Pastor."

With tears flowing down their cheeks, the Fords pointed to the little bundle behind them. The Indians bowed their heads and followed along behind the carriers—a sad little procession. Several hurried ahead to the little cemetery. When they arrived, a little grave had been dug in the hard, frozen ground. As the parents dismounted, the Indians from the mission received them with embraces and kisses.

After a short graveside ceremony, the Fords returned to their three-room adobe house. No longer did its whitewashed walls, bright curtains, or pretty dresser scarves laid on box furniture look cheerful. Together, they placed Teddy's toys and clothes in his little box bed. Orley tucked it far back in the corner, and Lillian covered it with a blanket. Then, sitting down on their cot, Orley took her hand and began to open his heart to her.

"Lillian, our plans are not always God's plans. Even though we had to surrender our precious baby boy, we may be sure that God is working out for us some higher good. In the future life we will see that our seemingly unanswered prayers and disappointed hopes have been among our greatest blessings. Whatever Christ asks us to give up, He offers in its stead something better."

For the first time in many days, Lillian saw hope.

"Something better," she said, pausing, then said it again. "Something better! I can't imagine anything better than Teddy. But I can trust God. Maybe He'll teach me how to do better work for Him or give me the energy and cheerfulness to do it." She spoke slowly, thoughtfully. "Maybe this great sorrow will bring us much closer to God and to each other. Maybe He can teach me to love this bleak, cold mountain country where our baby rests until Jesus comes. And I do want God to give me ways to show deeper love for these Indians."

"God's better gifts don't always seem good at the time, Lillian. I shall never forget a sentence I memorized years ago in college. Now I understand the meaning better. Would you like me to quote it?"

"Please do."

"Of all the gifts that heaven can bestow upon men, fellowship with Christ in His sufferings is the most weighty trust and the highest honor" (*The Desire of Ages*, p. 225).

Lillian looked puzzled. For several minutes she pondered each word. Only the sound of the cold wind and the ticking clock broke the silence. Tears began to flow again before she spoke. Orley held her close as she sobbed out her commitment.

"If suffering for Jesus' sake is one of His better gifts, I'm sure He'll help me believe that He knows what is best."

Chapter 2
Enemy Attacks

The Fords arrived at Pomata Mission in 1917 just a few months after their marriage. Soon, their home became a refuge for the sick and dying. Though thankful that they had taken a four-month course in practical medicine before coming to the Peruvian highlands, still they did not have adequate preparation for the problems they faced.

Early one morning, an Indian man knocked at their door with the simple request: "Come, my son has a sore foot."

Arriving at the hut, Orley looked with horror at a mangled and terribly swollen foot. One glance and the awful smell told him that gangrene had progressed to the knee. They carried the unconscious boy to the mission house.

"If I don't amputate his leg, he'll die," Orley said to Lillian.

"But you don't know how to do surgery," she objected.

"I know, but God does, and He can teach me. Start boiling water so I can sterilize our butcher knife and saw."

"You mean the one you use to saw wood?"

"I have nothing else. But first, let's pray."

In his first attempt, Orley didn't cut high enough. Later he tried again. Still dissatisfied with his work, he noted that too much of the bone stuck out. Though he'd never seen an amputation done, he declared the third operation a success. Using the same saw, he made the boy a wooden leg. Letters to friends in the U.S. brought a package containing adequate surgical instruments and a better wooden leg. Soon the boy learned to hobble all around the mission.

10 MISSION IN THE CLOUDS

God's blessings displayed at the clinic and the mission school convinced both Orley and Lillian that He keeps His promise of "something better." They loved teaching the converted Indians simple Bible truths, reading, writing, and arithmetic. Continual calls came for them to open new schools in the surrounding villages. Forced to send out native teachers with only three years of schooling, they marveled at how well God enabled them to read the Bible and avoid being cheated by the landowners in simple business transactions. But never were there enough teachers to answer the many calls.

"Come and look, Orley. I see lots of Indians coming toward our house," Lillian called. "I think they've been here before."

Orley went to the door and called his translator. Together they went to meet the delegation.

"We've come to get a teacher," demanded the leader. "And we won't go home without one."

"Have you met all the conditions?" Ford asked.

"Yes, all of them. We have built a schoolhouse and a house for the teacher. We have given up our vices, both alcohol and chewing coca leaf. Everything is ready."

They talked until Orley agreed to bring the teacher.

"You must bring Mrs. Ford too. We shall have a big feast."

With the new teacher, early the next morning they mounted their horses and followed the Indians over the rough mountain trail. Mile after mile, they picked their way among the rocks, keeping back from the steep precipices.

"How my toes and fingers ache from the cold!" Orley said. "Maybe we should dismount and walk to restore circulation."

So the Fords alternated between leading their horses over some of the more dangerous spots and riding until they couldn't stand the cold any longer. When they were still some distance from the village, a band of Indians met them, dressed in their best and bearing banners of welcome.

Finally the Indians escorted the Fords to a mud bench along the side of a room. The crowd sat outside on the ground, with their knees drawn up under their ponchos to keep warm.

Then came the feast. Soup, soup, and more soup of all kinds appeared, but always seasoned so hot that it burned all the

ENEMY ATTACKS 11

way down and for some time afterward. They also offered several kinds of potatoes and sheep milk to drink.

"Look, Orley," Lillian whispered. "There's a whole bird, minus the feathers, resting in that pot. The poor thing is staring up at us with great, death-filled eyes."

As they ate and visited, Orley noticed a mounting tension in the room. The Indians seemed unusually restless. Finally the old chief came close and said, "Maybe you had better go home. I will go with you."

They said goodbye to the teacher and followed the chief, wondering why he had left so quickly. The direction he went led them away from home.

"You're taking us the wrong way," Orley protested, but the old man pressed on, paying no attention to the missionary.

After they had left the village and were hidden by a small knoll, he finally turned and asked, "Did you hear the blowing of the horns while you were eating?"

"Yes, but why are we going the wrong direction?"

"Those horns called the people together to kill you. The priests and landowners do not want a school here. If I had not brought you this way, you would have met them on the road and never reached home. Now follow me quietly through a secret pass. We can get in front of the mob and go on safely."

He led them higher into the mountains to a big rock. Cautiously peering around it to the valley below, he said, "There they are, looking for you with clubs, slings, and stones."

The Fords peeked, too, noting the strategic place their enemies had planned to trap them. Every way of escape had been shut off. Orley bowed his head and prayed quietly.

"Thank you, God, for putting into the chief's heart a desire to protect us."

Quickly they progressed out of the valley and back to the trail toward home, far ahead of their enemies.

Thwarted in their plan to kill the missionaries, the angry Indians decided to destroy the schoolhouse and kill the teacher. Led by an Indian sorcerer, one dark night they planned to attack.

"First we must burn incense to win the favor of the spirits," the sorcerer instructed the mob of unruly Indians.

Somehow, while burning the incense, the sorcerer's hair and clothes caught on fire, and he was severely burned.

"Surely this is not a good sign," the enemies agreed. "We shall wait for a more favorable night."

Several weeks later, on a dark, stormy night, they gathered again to make final plans for the attack. Suddenly a bolt of lightning struck and killed the sorcerer's child.

"The spirits seem against us! We must postpone our attack," they concluded.

Undaunted, they met again. With firebrands to burn the schoolhouse, the large crowd moved forward on their cruel mission. Before they could set fire to the school's grass roof, they had to pass by a field of ripe, standing barley. Sparks from their brands caught in the dry grain. Thwarted again from their evil plans, the crowd tried to put the fire out. But the large field of barley burned up completely.

Still undaunted, the wicked men met the fourth time. The ringleader said, "Every attack we've made has ended in failure. Let's spy on the teacher to see if we can find the cause. I suggest we go to one of the teacher's prayer meetings to see if he's working with the spirits to cause us trouble."

Creeping close to the schoolhouse, the ringleader listened to the meeting. At the close, he heard the teacher pray.

"God, You know many attempts have been made to destroy our schoolhouse. You know our enemies do not understand they are really hurting You. Especially bless their leader with Your love and care. Amen."

That prayer touched the leader's heart. He not only became a friend of the teacher, but also began to attend the meetings.

The Holy Spirit changed that man. God used him to lead most of the village to accept the good news of Jesus' love.

Sometimes, the Fords learned, God's promises of "something better" take longer because of wicked people. After a new school opened in another village, the enemies of progress threatened to kill the first child who dared enter.

The day that the school opened, one little boy begged his parents, "Please, let me go. I want so much to learn."

"But you know how cruel some of the village folk can be," they replied with fear.

"I'm not afraid."

Reluctantly, they consented. As the little fellow returned home, several older Indian boys caught him in a narrow gully and stoned him to death.

Returning home from the churchyard where they'd buried him, his brokenhearted parents were attacked by men led by the village priest. They beat the father until he could no longer walk. Because of this cruelty, soldiers eventually came to guard the school. Soon many children attended, and the sacrifice of one little Indian boy resulted in his friends receiving the Christian education he had wanted so badly.

Persecution continued in other villages. The mission Indians refused to pay for a drunken feast, so the mob burned the schoolhouse and the teacher's home and tried to kill the teacher and his wife. But God enjoys doing for His children what He did for His own Son, Jesus. They escaped through the crowd without being seen.

Goaded on by the anger of the priest, the mob burned the home of each family that helped establish the school, and stole all their livestock. Worse still, the mob either burned or stole their small children. With everything they possessed gone, these poor Indians fled to the mission station for protection.

"I will go immediately to the local authorities to demand justice for this terrible abuse," Ford said.

Sad to say, even the higher officials seldom kept their promises of justice. These brave Christian Indians tried to return to their village, but armed bands drove them away.

"Are you sorry you chose to follow Christ?" Ford asked the refugee Indians on the day twenty of them were baptized.

"We're sorry we lost our homes, our little children, and our cattle, but we're glad we can hear God's Word every day. We're so happy that the children we have left can go to the mission school to learn Jesus' way."

"Now I understand," Lillian said to Orley when they returned home. "Sometimes, only suffering enables us to receive God's gift of something better."

Chapter 3
The Call to Ecuador

The Fords had worked with and loved the Quechua and Aymara Indians at Pomata Mission for four years. Only fifty Christian Indians had greeted them when they arrived. Now 400 baptized Indians not only loved Jesus but practiced a better way of life. Eight native teachers conducted school at the mission, plus seven others in out-schools.

Ford rejoiced in the statement of a Peruvian senator, "You Seventh-day Adventists have done more to educate the Indians in fifteen years than the state church ever did in 400 years."

The year 1921 brought big changes in Orley and Lillian's lives. First, a new baby boy, which they named Elden, arrived. But Orley and Lillian's health suffered from the high altitude. Both had enlarged hearts, and their deficient diet resulted in infected gums. Orley developed stomach ulcers. Lillian, thin and pale, turned blue when they crossed the high mountain passes.

"I wish we could take a vacation at lower altitude and get to feeling better," Lillian said to Orley as he brought in the mail from the Lake Titicaca mail boat. "I've felt so tired since Elden's birth."

"Good idea! I'll write to the leaders at the Inca Union Mission and suggest that we need a change," he said as he sorted the mail. "Why, here's a letter from them."

He opened it and quickly scanned the contents.

"They've suggested a change, but not a vacation," he said.

THE CALL TO ECUADOR 15

"Orley, tell me what the letter says."

He read aloud. "For some time, we have been looking for the ideal couple who could pioneer the work among the Indians of Ecuador. Nothing has been done for the thousands of Indians in the Andes highlands of that country. The mission board has prayed much for guidance and unanimously decided to ask you. Could you begin preparation to make the trip from Peru to Ecuador as soon as possible?"

"Are they asking us to move from our comfortable home and our well-organized mission with a new baby?" Lillian interrupted.

"More than that, my dear. The government of Ecuador has fought the entrance of the Bible into that country with a hatred bordering on fanaticism. The troubles we've faced here will seem small compared to what is in store for us. The state church will stir up opposition against any foreigners who challenge their system of tyranny over the Indians of Ecuador."

"Will we be alone, Orley?"

"If you're referring to other missionaries, yes, at first. But if you are talking about God and the angels, no. Always remember, dear. When God calls, He's already made plans for something better."

Lillian looked out the window at the schoolchildren working with their teacher on their garden plots. "How can we tell these dear people that we must leave them?" she thought aloud.

Orley stepped across the room and took her hand. "Then you'll go?"

Though her eyes had filled with tears, she looked up at him and said, "I'll go anywhere with you and God."

The long trip began with the lake steamer to Puno. The train took them to the rest home in Arequipa. Lillian prayed much that night for baby Elden, remembering that here, little Teddy had died. Another day on the train brought them to the port of Mollendo, where they boarded a ship to take them north. For eight days they traveled up the desertlike coast of Peru to the Guayas River in central Ecuador.

"How beautiful! What a change!" Lillian exclaimed.

"Yes, from brown to the luxuriant green," Orley agreed. "Look at those multicolored birds in the banana trees." Together, they watched the river pilot who would guide their steamship to the port of Guayaquil come aboard.

Travel in 1921 was often difficult and uncomfortable. Detained in that muddy, mosquito-ridden, steaming city for several days, the Fords waited to make train connections to Quito in the highlands. The night before the train left, a river launch took them across the muddy river and nearer to the railroad station. Early the next morning, they hoped to get seats on the crowded train.

Hotel beds used boards in place of springs. Despite mosquito netting, mosquitoes pestered them all night. Insufficient water pressure didn't even provide a trickle on the second floor. To get relief from the hot, stuffy hotel room, Orley suggested they take a short walk.

"But if we take the baby, I'm afraid he'll wake up." Lillian objected. "He'll be all right. I'll lock the door."

When they returned half an hour later, Orley put the key in the lock, and discovered that the door was unlocked.

"That's strange," he said. "I know I locked it."

"The baby's gone!" Lillian shrieked.

"Let's get the hotel manager to help us find him." Orley turned and ran down the stairs two at a time, with Lillian not far behind.

"I don't know anything about your baby," the manager said.

Frantic with fear, they rushed from room to room, asking everyone. No one had seen their three-month-old baby.

"What's that little shack in the back?" Orley asked.

"Oh, that's the kitchen for the hotel," the manager replied.

With hope almost gone, Orley ran to the open door. There sat the cook on the floor, with little Elden gulping contentedly at her ample breast.

She beamed with delight, explaining, "Your poor child would have starved to death if I had not rescued him in time."

Lillian never let her baby out of her sight after that. As they resumed their journey, they noted stark contrasts from their train windows. Gaping precipices, majestic mountains eternally covered with snow, great glaciers, and volcanoes belching out ashes and smoke rose above the squalid huts of the Indians. Used like beasts of burden by the rich landowners, the Indians were condemned to a drudgery that crushed out all hope of release. At every station, beggars swarmed around the train, pleading for help.

"I've never seen such human misery! If only we could help them all," Lillian sighed.

Finally they arrived at Quito, the capital, built on a plateau almost two miles above sea level and surrounded by snow-capped peaks. Orley observed, "What a beautiful old city with its red roofs and colonial architecture! Look at the church spires! If only the people knew the God to whom those spires point."

They stayed in Quito for a few months while Orley prayed and hunted for a mission site to begin work among the Indians. Finally he decided on the valley surrounding Lake Colta. Here on this high, cold plain, surrounded by magnificent snowcapped mountains and great glaciers, about 20,000 Indians lived in squalid huts surrounding the lake.

The Fords retraced their journey by train to Riobamba and hired oxcarts to take them and their belongings up the hill to the lake.

"You won't like the filthy, thatch-roofed, mud-walled hut I had to rent for our home," Orley explained. "It's been used as a saloon, but I couldn't find anything better. I hope the owner has emptied it for our arrival as he promised."

"I can clean it up tomorrow," Lillian said. "I just hope we make it before dark. It's already late afternoon."

"Oh, no!" Orley gasped, as they made a turn in the road. "The yard and house are full of drunken, bleary-eyed Indians! I forgot that today is the feast of Saint Anthony." Ahead of them, an image of St. Anthony sat on a rickety table between a drummer and some dancers."

Lillian shuddered as she looked at the black hole that was to be the entrance to her new home. "How will we ever put up our beds in that mess?"

Orley turned and looked back down the hill. "I don't see the oxcart that has our beds. Lillian, I'll have to go back and find it. No doubt the driver needs help to push and pull it over the steep places."

"But you can't leave the baby and me here alone!"

"I have to, dear, or we'll never get our things tonight. God will send His angels to protect you. Just keep trusting and praying. I'll come back as soon as I can."

Terrified, the young mother watched her husband disappear in the deepening twilight. Moments later, a drunken Indian pushed himself close to her and tried to grab her hand to kiss it, all the while calling her pet names. She climbed onto the oxcart, pushing him away. Several others joined him, throwing her kisses and making very ungraceful bows. With their hats cocked over one ear, they staggered around her, trying to touch her.

"God, protect me," she prayed, her heart pounding in fear.

One by one, her admirers slumped down on the cold ground in drunken stupors. The old drum boomed on, but the dancers fell, huddled together by cactus plants. Anxiously, she looked down the road but could see nothing in the darkness. Just then, a half-breed Indian grabbed a guitar and came close to play for her. His strange tunes and lewd gestures added to the terror of her thoughts.

"What if something happens to Orley? I can't stay here alone with this drunken man. I have no friends. I can't speak the language, nor can I trust these strange people. Why, God, did You send me to this awful place?" But Lillian could do nothing but wait and believe that He who had sent her there had power to keep her safe.

Chapter 4
Mission Miracles

Somewhere in the darkness, Lillian's keen ears caught a new sound, the creak of an oxcart. She tuned out the ugly music of the drunken man and listened intently.

Faintly, she heard the voice she loved so much. "I'm coming, Lillian!"

Her heart pounded wildly as she climbed from her perch, clutched her baby close, and ran into Orley's open arms. "I can endure even the most impossible situation when I'm with you," she whispered.

"You may have to tonight," he said. "Let's push our way past this drunken fellow and find a place for our beds."

What they saw by the dim light of the fire made them shudder. Chickens roosted above their heads, and guinea pigs dodged their feet. Dogs and pigs slept in the corners. Smoke from the open fire filled the room, and strings of soot fell from the roof every time a gust of wind blew in. A few drunken Indians, unable to go home, moaned and groaned in their misery on the muddy floor. The foul odor made Lillian feel sick.

"We must get these oxcarts inside, or everything will be stolen by morning," Orley said. "Since there's no outside gate, we'll drive them through the house and into the corral."

Fortunately, most of the other animals joined the six oxen, but a few roosters stayed by to crow at intervals by their beds. Neither Lillian, Orley, or the baby, slept much that night.

If curious visitors in the form of their Indian neighbors

hadn't walked in unannounced, they wouldn't have known morning had come. The darkness inside the hut made it impossible to cook, read, write, or do any work without a lamp.

"Our first job is to transform this place into something livable. I suggest we begin by cutting a window in the side," Orley said. "I'll try to hire someone to help me. Would you like to have the walls replastered and whitewashed?"

"Plus the soot swept away and mats put up for a ceiling and a floor covering," Lillian added.

What a change! People came from near and far to admire their clean one-room home. They inspected everything, especially the Fords' typewriter, folding cots, and kerosene stove. However, the first rain drenched everything. The thatched roof, which had been drying all summer, offered no more protection than a tree. Black, sooty water poured through the mats, soaking their beds, food, and books until there wasn't a dry spot in the house.

Huddled together under an umbrella in the dampness and cold, Lillian complained, "Surely this isn't the 'something better' that God promised."

Trying to speak positively, Orley reminded her, "At least the Indians are still selling us their produce. Today we bought milk, eggs, barley, and potatoes."

But as the weeks went by, that stopped as well. The priests forbade the Indians to have any contact with the hated missionaries. No little faces pushed tight against their one window. No raps were heard on the door. No pleading voices of the sick called, "Doctorcito, help."

"You must get out of my house!" the landlord demanded.

"No," Orley objected. "I've paid the rent for six months, and you signed the contract before witnesses."

"But I hear that forty men have sworn they will burn down the house. You're a curse to the country. We don't want our soil polluted by heretics. The priest says you came here to get rich by robbing us."

"Did we not treat all the sick who came to us and give them free medicine? Did we charge to pull the teeth?" Orley asked.

"The devil works through your treatments. They won't

bring lasting cures. Go!" he shouted in fear. "Or the curse of heaven will fall on us."

Later, six half-drunken Indians came demanding medicine. "What is your sickness?" Orley asked.

Immediately, they became angry and unreasonable. Sensing they had come to drive the Fords from their home, Orley maneuvered the unsteady fellows outside and shut the door.

Living alone among such violent enemies, the young missionaries pleaded with God, "Father, the priests and the landholders, who exploit these Indians, have convinced them that they must get rid of us. But You can thwart their plots to burn our home and kill us. Grant us a miracle, God, to change the attitudes of these poor, frightened Indians."

Instead, the anger of the Indians increased. None of the grain they had planted grew. Looking at their dry, parched fields, the priest shouted, "As long as these devils remain in our country, it will not rain. I hereby curse the fields until you drive them out."

Certain that their children would die for lack of barley and potatoes, they came to the Fords, pleading, "You've lived beside us for several months. We've seen nothing bad in you, but to save us from starvation, please go."

"Orley," Lillian said after they left, "I feel impressed that this drought is God's way of granting both us and them something better. Let's invite our neighbors to join us in praying for rain."

"Good idea! I'll go out and invite them to our home."

About fifty Indians responded. Crowding into the one room, they crouched on the floor, fearing they had placed themselves on the devil's ground. None dared look up as Orley spoke.

"You are very brave to come here hoping to save your crops. The only One who can send the rain or keep it back is the same God who sent us to live among you. He loves you. He died for you and cares for you now. If you will kneel with us, we will ask our God to send rain."

And God, who loves to do more than we can ask or think, sent heavy rain that night, which drenched their parched fields. The rains kept on until the people thought they might have to ask the missionary to stop the rain. But God had yet another miracle to help these Indians learn to trust the Fords instead of the priest.

Ecuadorian Indians love bullfights. At one of their feasts in the open space in front of the church, a bull gored a woman. Its horn ripped open her face from her scalp to her chin, tearing one eye from its socket.

"Let's call Mr. Ford at once," her family suggested.

"No! No!" the priest shouted. "She's going to die. Do not ruin her chance of salvation by permitting that heretic to come into your home."

So they let her lie on the ground all night, making no attempt to give her first aid. The next morning they found her alive but very weak from shock and loss of blood.

"She's not dead yet," her husband said. "Let's call Ford in spite of what the priest says."

When Orley looked at the victim lying there in the blood and filth, with one eye hanging out, he knew she was nearly dead from shock. If he sewed up the wound, would gangrene set in?

Turning to the crowd around her, he said, "Please join me while I kneel beside this woman and pray that the Master Physician will guide my hands."

After carrying the unconscious woman inside, he cleansed her wounds, removed broken pieces of cheekbone, replaced the eye that had hung out of her head overnight, and closed the wound with fifteen stitches. All the while, the onlookers made bets on when the women would die, but they paused to listen when Orley prayed again that God's name be glorified.

God not only healed the woman but restored the sight in the eye. Convinced that the missionaries, not the angry priest, were their true friends, crowds began to change their one-room hut into a hospital and clinic. Waiting sick gathered by 5:00 a.m. The stone by the front door became the dental chair.

"And today our little home became a chapel." Lillian smiled at Orley. "Those poor Indians tried so hard to sing 'Jesus Loves Me' with us. Won't it be wonderful when they give their hearts to God so He can take away their horrible vices and give them the wonderful surprises He has for them?"

Chapter 5
Challenge at Colta Mission

"We can't continue to serve these people in this crowded hut," Orley stated with finality. "We must find a suitable location for a permanent mission."

"You know how the priests and the wealthy Ecuadorian landowners hate us because of our influence over the Indians," Lillian responded. "No Indian would dare sell us land."

"I know, but we do have God on our side and . . ."

"He always offers something better," they said in unison. Laughing together, they clasped hands and lifted them heavenward.

"Well, what are you waiting for, Mr. Missionary? Go out and find God's special plan. Maybe you should take money with you, just in case this is the day for 'something better.' I'll have dinner ready when you return."

Several hours later, a jubilant Orley burst into their hut.

"He did it, Lillian! A widow offered us that piece of land we've been eyeing on the hillside about half a mile from the lake."

"The one with all the lava rock that we could use in building?"

"Right, but her price was out of reason. She said she had to have extra money to give to the priest so he wouldn't excommunicate her for selling it to us. But I kept bargaining with her. And guess what? Lillian, she signed the papers. The money is paid. We own the land!"

"What? Only God could do an impossibility like that in this land of *mañana*. I'm so glad you have everything finalized before the news gets out."

But the next day, trouble began.

The news leaked out, and the seller immediately became an outcast, excommunicated from her church. No one would sell to her or buy from her. Though very sympathetic with her troubles, the Fords knew God had directed in the purchase of this land and prayed He would solve her problems too.

Anxious to move from their miserable hut before the rainy season began, they immediately hired men to begin excavation for the foundation. Lumber had to be brought up from the coast and hauled from the railroad to the property in the Fords' cart drawn by two cows. Orley and Lillian worked long hours, squeezing in time to build despite the crowds of sick that demanded treatment.

One morning, shortly before their new house was ready to occupy, Orley awoke, moaning, "Lillian, I have an awful pain on my lower right side."

"You look flushed. Let me take your temperature." She put the thermometer in his mouth. "Orley," she said after looking at it, "You're very sick. If only we could get medical help!"

Several days of high fever and pain, symptoms of appendicitis, made them consider going to the United States for surgery. But if they left then, not only would the property be damaged and the materials stolen, but the people would assume they had accepted defeat and abandoned the mission.

Turning to God in faith, they pleaded, "God, we're in trouble. You promised never to leave us or forsake us. We need healing so we can continue to do the work You gave us. And we also need water. You know we're building on a hill half a mile from the lake. Please help us to find clean, pure water."

A few days later, Orley not only felt well enough to again supervise construction, but he also hired Indians to begin digging a well. When they reached a depth of forty feet, they stopped.

Discouraged, Orley poured out his woes to Lillian. "I've offered them wages far beyond anything they could ever earn, and still they refuse to dig anymore. They fear they'll disturb the spirits of the dead, or the wall will cave in and bury them, or they'll catch pneumonia from the cool air."

"Trust God, Orley," Lillian said with a smile, "and wait for something better to happen."

A few days later, an Indian from another village offered to dig just one more meter. "If there's no water then, I will dig no more."

Many times that day, Orley went to the well to check. "Have you struck water?" he called.

From the depths came the dismal answer, "No."

The next day the Indian dug again. "I've almost finished my meter and still no water!" he shouted to the anxious missionaries.

Surrounded by skeptical Indians who sneered, "You'll never get water from a dry hill," Orley and Lillian bowed their heads. "Father, we need another miracle. Show them Your power."

A short time later, they heard a shout from down in the well. Rushing to the spot, they heard the digger exclaim, "There's already a puddle of water in the bottom and more coming in rapidly."

Crowds came to wonder at the "witchery" that the missionaries called "a gift from their God." When Orley installed a pump and brought the water to the surface, they shook their heads in amazement and begged, "Come, find water for us. We are weary of carrying it up steep hills to our homes."

As soon as the Fords had finished one room, they gladly left their dark hut. Gradually, they made progress on the other three rooms, plastering the ceilings and walls with mud over and over again, smoothing it evenly and covering it with whitewash. Lillian worked especially hard finishing the bedroom. The day after she completed putting up the bed, hanging curtains, and arranging furniture, their little girl, Arlis Elizabeth, arrived.

But another arrival caused much more stir among the Indians. Months before, the Fords had ordered an automobile from the United States, which now arrived in boxes. Fortunately, Orley's mechanical aptitude and experience enabled him to bolt the Model T Ford car together. Bearing the license plate number 1, he took it over the rough roads, dodging Indians and burros, who either stood stock-still in the middle of the road, climbed the steep banks, hid in the deep gorges, or, like rabbits, ran ahead, too frightened to turn aside.

Returning from a trip to town, Orley laughingly explained, "Some say there's a devil inside, others think it's propelled by angels, and many kneel beside it to pray. But the boys climb all over it, giving the strangest explanations of how it runs. The jealous priest threatened them with excommunication if they rode in it."

"Has that stopped them from stealing rides?" Lillian asked.

"Not at all. I'm sure curiosity and the fun of jumping on the spare tire or running boards far exceeds their fears of eternal punishment. But I did have fun 'heaping coals of fire' on our enemy when two men, carrying heavy bundles, asked for a ride," chuckled Orley.

"I do recall the priest made a decree that any thing or person that had been in the 'devil's car' would be excommunicated. So what was in the bundles?" Lillian asked.

"An image, the priest's vesture, and other 'sacred' articles being transferred from one church to another. Though my hitchhikers objected vehemently, I drove straight to the priest's door. You should have seen his face when I handed him the defiled objects." Orley laughed again.

A few days later, when Orley returned from a town trip to purchase supplies, he had a very different kind of story to tell Lillian. "While there, a sudden downpour turned the streams into swollen torrents," he said. "I waited several hours, then cautiously attempted the drive home. Just as I started to cross an old stone bridge, two horsemen pushed their way ahead of me. I slammed on the brakes and watched them. Before the second one reached the other side, the bridge collapsed, dumping him into the swirling waters. Quickly I shut off the motor and with the other rider tried to rescue him. But he was dead when we found his body."

"I'm sorry," Lillian answered, and then with a shudder she added, "What if you had crossed first?"

"I thought of that all the way home. Without God's protection we couldn't even do the simplest everyday tasks."

"You're so right, Orley, we'll probably never know how many times He has intervened these three years in Ecuador." Lillian looked concerned. "But Orley, I can see that living with constant stress is aggravating your stomach ulcers. You're losing weight. I'm glad we're due for a furlough soon and that relief missionaries will fill in for us."

"But we've accomplished so little. The lack of response from these degraded Indians is far different from the way the Peruvian Indians crowded into our churches and schools." Orley's voice sounded sad. "They're so steeped in superstitious ignorance, they don't want a better life. To be considered a man, an Indian feels he must get drunk at least once a week and on all feast days."

"Yes, all they want from us is medical care, usually from their drunken brawls—fingers bitten off, heads cut open, noses broken. Not one has yet given his heart to Jesus," Lillian added.

"So we'll prepare to meet their needs and leave the rest to God. We must take advantage of that six-month course in medical training offered at Loma Linda while we're in the States. I feel a need for more knowledge in that area," Orley said.

After seven years in the Andes highlands, four in Peru, and three in Ecuador, the Fords, with little Elden and one-year-old Arlis, returned home. After completing the medical training, the doctor insisted that Orley spend a month in bed, recovering from his ulcers and gaining a needed forty pounds. Lillian left Elden with Grandma Ford and took little Arlis to see her relatives in Kansas.

While there the baby became ill with an infection. Lillian took her to a hospital in Wichita, where she had the best of care. However, during this time of crisis, her lungs, weakened and expanded by the high altitude in Ecuador, collapsed, and she died at nineteen months.

Orley and Elden arrived for the funeral. A little grave in Peru and now this one in Kansas told of the sacrifices that these brave missionaries made for the God they love.

Chapter 6
Turmoil, Trust, Peace

With sad hearts the Fords returned to the mission by Lake Colta. Not even the beauty of the lake and the magnificent snowcapped mountains could ease the hurt. When their freight arrived, which had been shipped before baby Arlis's death, they cried together as they unpacked the little dresses and toys. The big doll, which Elden called "Arlis," became his dearest treasure and constant companion even while he slept.

The never-ending stream of sick Indians, from dawn till dark, helped divert the minds of the grief-stricken parents from their sorrow.

"Orley, I'd like to start a school. Might help me think of something besides Baby Arlis," Lillian decided. "Let's urge every person that comes to the mission to send their boys and girls."

"Don't be discouraged if you don't get any pupils," he warned.

Each parent objected with, "Oh, no, our children can't learn to read like white children. They are like little burros."

But Lillian persisted. Though thousands of Indians lived around the lake, only two brave boys arrived the day school opened. Later, little Luis Lemus came only on rainy days. His father made him work in the fields on sunny days.

"Your boy can never learn to read that way," Lillian explained.

"My boy will either work or leave home," he shouted angrily.

"Please let me stay with you and work for you so I can go to school," Luis pleaded with his teacher. She consented.

Luis not only loved the missionaries but, while living with them, also learned to love their God. The boy changed so much that his amazed father admitted, "This new religion has made my boy obedient. He can come home and go to school too."

Two years later, Luis and his father became the first converts among the Colta Indians.

"We've prayed and waited for this joyous event for five years," Orley said.

Lillian's school grew. That Christmas, hundreds of Indians attended the school program instead of the Christmas mass. Furious, the priest threatened the missionaries. A few days later, Orley received an urgent request to investigate a theft down by the lake.

"Sanchez," he said to his native helper and translator. "Since you understand what will be said, please go for me."

Soon a man came shouting, "Sanchez has been thrown in the lake and is drowning!"

Orley dashed to his Model T Ford and drove to the lake. He saw two wealthy landowners whom he had treated when sick standing among the Indians. Thinking they would help him, he hurried toward them.

With vulgar oaths, one struck him with a long whip while the other hit Ford on the head with an iron bar, cutting him deeply and knocking him unconscious.

When he came to, friendly Indians had dragged him to the water's edge and bathed his bloody face. In addition to the gash on his head, he had a broken nose, a finger nearly severed, and bruises all over his body. Probably the pith helmet he wore saved him from death. Meanwhile, Sanchez, a strong swimmer, had escaped.

If Orley had not restrained them, hundreds of Indians would have taken revenge for the cruelty given their beloved "Doctorcito" (dear doctor). A few days later, an Indian came to him with a strange lump in his leg.

"What's this?" Ford asked.

"The bullet my boss shot at you, only it hit me instead," he answered.

Orley kept the bullet as a reminder of God's love and protection.

Not satisfied, Ford's enemies sent accusations to the president of Ecuador. He was accused of being: (1) A "quack" doctor causing many deaths; (2) a Peruvian spy; and (3) an unlicensed lawyer. After summoning Orley to Quito, the president curtly ordered him to get out of the country in one week or go to jail.

With much prayer, hundreds of people who knew the Fords signed a petition pointing out: (1) Mrs. Ford conducts a free elementary school for Indian children; (2) by his medical skills, Mr. Ford has saved a large number of people from death; (3) he answers calls for help at any hour of the day or night; (4) an experienced midwife, Mrs. Ford has saved many an Indian mother and baby; (5) Mr. Ford does not exploit the people but is useful, necessary, and kind.

A short time later, a courteous and apologetic president sent for Ford. "I had been misinformed. My greatest desire is that you remain with us, serving the Lake Colta Indians. As a physician, I shall personally grant you permission to practice."

Again, God battled victoriously with Ford's enemies.

Sometime later, Orley rejoiced that he had a knowledge of obstetrics. Without doctor or nurse, he helped bring his own little daughter, Sylvia, into the world. Now Elden, with his new little sister asleep in her buggy, went to school with the Indian children. Lillian's schoolwork, plus helping in the clinic and teaching Elden English at home, kept her more than busy.

For seven years, the Fords had lived within three miles of Cajabamba, a town of almost 2,000 Spanish people. Everyone knew them, for they had treated the sick in almost every home and shopped at the marketplace.

"I'm convinced we live near the most corrupt town along the railroad." Orley said. "As I've learned to know these people and become aware of their crimes, I've felt an urgent desire to offer them the gospel of love."

"But who would rent us a meeting place in this hate-filled town?" Lillian asked.

"Only God, who specializes in the impossible, can arrange

that. Let's pray, and then I'll go to town and make a few inquiries."

He met a man facing a lawsuit who needed money immediately.

"I'll rent you a room in my two-story house. Let's settle on the date you want possession. If you'll give me the money now, I'll sign the contract," he said.

Unknown to Ford, he forged his wife's name on the contract, received the money, and left town. When the time arrived, Ford went to get the key.

"You cannot have the key!" the frantic woman shouted. "I can't bring upon my family the curse of heaven and the black eye of the church!"

"But I have the contract. Please let us enter peacefully. I don't want to call the town officials and force an entrance."

"No! No!" she shouted. "Down with the Protestants! Long live our religion!"

When the first night of meetings arrived, the whole town turned out, but not to hear the sermon. They shouted curses on anyone who ventured to go inside. The landlady had hired a band to play strange tunes in the doorway. Ford noticed that many people in whose homes he had spent entire nights treating their sick were the first to cast insulting remarks.

Every night for two months they met taunts and jeers. Their largest attendance on any night was five and the average attendance was three. One of the worst fellows in town, a drunk, appeared night after night, each time cleaner and more alert. Instead of rejoicing at the transformation in his life, this man's family turned him out without mercy, threatening his life. After his baptism, he became a colporteur and later married Sanchez's daughter. God blessed the books and Bibles he sold far beyond the Lake Colta area.

"Something unheard of in Ecuador has happened!" Orley ran to the school to share the news with Lillian. "Several families from San Miguel in the province of Bolivar have sent word asking for someone to come and teach them."

"Wonderful!" Lillian exclaimed. "How will we answer their call?"

"I'll send Sanchez and his family right away, and we'll follow later to hold meetings and treat the sick. One man offered them a place to stay at his house."

On July 4, 1929, they loaded their car with food, and started out on a high, narrow, almost impassable road. Arriving at dusk, Lillian suggested, "Orley, I'll need water. While I take care of baby Sylvia, could you and Elden go to the town square and get some?"

Unknown to Ford, the townspeople had purposely turned off the water so they'd fall into a trap. A boy stepped forward, saying, "If you'll go down that street, you'll find a gully where there's a spring of water."

Taking Elden's hand, Ford hesitated, thinking, "I don't like going down this dark, narrow place. But we do need water."

Suddenly, from out of the darkness, they heard a shot. Then another and another. Orley counted about eight or ten shots, but not one touched them.

Meanwhile, Lillian heard one lone tap of the church bell, usually a call for the people to gather for an attack. Could this affect her husband and son? she wondered. As she cared for the baby, her feelings of fear grew. Suddenly the Sanchez girl burst into the room, screaming, "Mr. Ford and your son have been shot!"

In that instant, Lillian began to panic. Was she alone with her baby among an angry mob who had just killed her husband and son? A second later, words she had read that morning came to her mind: "I, even I, am he who comforts you. Who are you that you fear mortal men?" (Isaiah 51:12, NIV).

Filled with courage, she grabbed Sylvia, wrapped her in a blanket, and ran to a group of women at the corner of the street.

"What's happened?" she demanded. "Has my husband been killed?"

Some shrugged their shoulders. Others grunted, "Perhaps."

Frantic, she dashed to the Sanchez home. Together, they knelt in prayer. Again she set out to find her dear ones. As she neared the town plaza, she saw her husband and boy being escorted by the town officials, followed by a cursing mob.

With deep gratitude for God's deliverance, they locked the door to their room, hoping to get some rest. But at 10:00 p.m., they heard the shout, "Kill the Protestants!" Rocks pelted the only door, and bullets made little holes in the thin panels. Eventually larger rocks broke through the wood and landed on the floor. They piled the big tables and sofa over the holes.

Orley gathered his little family around him in a corner protected by the thick adobe walls and began quoting Psalm 46. "God is our refuge and strength, a very present help in trouble. Therefore we will not fear" (verses 1, 2).

Listening to these promises quoted by the man she loved gave Lillian peace, even though the bombardment continued for over half an hour. Rocks of every size covered the floor and broke almost all the furniture. Bullets kept bouncing off the wall. Alone and unarmed, the little family knew angels protected them as they prayed and claimed God's promises. Baby Sylvia slept through it all, and Elden was too scared to make a sound. Then they heard the shout, "Let's burn the heretics!"

While the mob ran to get kerosene and matches, the town officials came, pretending to protect them. Soldiers arrived the next day, but even then, shots were fired into the room each night. No one would sell them food, so after three days, they realized they could do nothing to bring the gospel to the people of San Miguel.

Still, Orley refused to give up. Sending the Sanchez family back to Lake Colta, he moved Lillian and the children to a hotel in a nearby town. Going about on horseback, he visited the interested people who had fled to the country.

While he was gone, the wife of the hotel owner came to Lillian. "We cannot have a Protestant devil living here. You must leave at once."

Where could she go? She knew no one. She shot up a prayer for help. An old man who stayed at the hotel heard what had happened. He stepped up to her and said, "I have a sister who has an extra room in her home."

Lillian felt impressed to trust him. Quickly she gathered up her things, put them in the Ford, and followed him.

When Orley returned, he found the hotel room barred and empty.

Hurrying to the manager, he demanded, "Where are my wife and family?"

"I don't know," he answered.

Frantically, Orley searched throughout the village, inquiring everywhere. Finally he found the little house where they stayed.

Filled with relief, he dropped into a chair, exclaiming, "I know God wants us here! It seems as if we're in the middle of the great controversy between Christ and the devil. But in each battle, Christ gives the victory. I've been giving Bible studies to two most eager listeners. One man, a murderer, is probably the most feared man in this country, but already, God is transforming him into a meek, lovable person. The other man's wife has left him, declaring he cannot even see his children. But he's so in love with Jesus that he's requested baptism anyway."

"Then this ordeal hasn't been in vain." Lillian smiled at Orley. "And each new crisis has strengthened my faith in God's power to grant us something better. I've experienced a peace in trusting God that I could never have known otherwise."

"Me too. Who knows? Perhaps these two transformed men will do more for the gospel of Christ than we could have done had we been allowed to remain."

And so it proved. A year later, the man's wife and children accepted Jesus and they became a happy, united family. The murderer, intent on killing his enemy, became so filled with love that he stepped from his hiding place, extended his hand, and asked forgiveness. News spread about the power of this new religion, and many began to respect the Protestant God

Chapter 7
Adventures Galore!

Thankful to be back at Lake Colta, the Fords plunged into their usual busy routine. One evening, Orley came home with concern etched in his face.

"Today, friendly Indians warned me of a plan to kill all the white population and set up a government that will give justice to the Indians," he said.

"I don't believe these downtrodden, submissive people are capable of such a thing!" Lillian replied.

But several days later, they heard that government soldiers had crushed a revolt in a village ten miles from Colta. Because of the unrest, a cavalry battalion had been stationed across the lake from their home.

That day, friends from the mission office at Quito came to visit the Fords.

"I must go to town for supplies," Orley said to his friend. "Shall we take the children and give the two ladies a chance to chat in peace?"

As they drove by a flock of sheep drinking from the lake, Orley commented, "How I wish the Indians only drank lake water like those sheep. We're in the midst of the Feast of the Three Wise Men, which means heavy drinking and plenty of trouble."

They finished their business and got into the car to start for home. Suddenly they heard shouts and screams and saw people with guns running into the streets. White refugees fled into town, driving their few animals and carrying whatever possessions they had grabbed in haste. Moments later, thousands of yelling Indians filled the mountainsides, waving clubs, knives, and lances.

"Quick, we must try to get home to protect our wives and the mission!"

A short way from town, soldiers stopped them. "Turn back!" they shouted. "They'll kill you if you go on!"

Ignoring the warning, Ford drove on until he met the village priest. "Don't try to make the pass. Those drunken Indians are out for blood! I saw them take the animals of the landowners, cut out their hearts, and string them on posts, shouting, 'That's the fate of the first white person we can get our hands on.' They won't even have mercy on their friends."

As the priest talked, angry Indians began streaming through the pass. Flying stones began to bounce off the car. They faced the mob on a steep grade, too narrow to turn the car around, with a high mountain wall on one side and a deep precipice on the other.

"Hold on and pray. I've got to back down!" Orley shouted.

The narrow road definitely sloped to the canyon side with only a foot or two to spare. On several sharp curves, he almost backed over the side. Stones kept raining from above. A large one went through the top of the car and landed between the two men. Just before the Indians came near enough to use their clubs and knives, the missionaries came to a wide spot in the road. Quickly Ford turned around and sped ahead as fast as he dared to safety.

As soon as he arrived in town, he telephoned the governor of the province, asking for more soldiers to protect the mission, though he had heard rumors that it was already in flames. Shortly, reinforcements arrived, rushed in by trucks. Finally, the soldiers told Ford, "You may proceed cautiously. Look for traps along the road."

Terrible sights awaited them. The dead and wounded were strewn over the bare hills.

"Look, Daddy," Elden shouted. "There's a deep trench cut in the road. It's right where we started to back down the hill. God saved us just in time."

ADVENTURES GALORE! 37

Carefully they made their way around it, thanking God for His protection for them. "Please do the same for the women and the mission," they prayed.

Meanwhile, Lillian and her friend, the only white persons left among the Indians, watched as the poncho-clad men rushed down the mountain slopes with poles and knives, eager to rebel against their hated masters. Lillian recognized many of them as friends who had often been to the mission and stopped them.

"Please go home," she begged. "Don't make yourselves targets for the soldiers."

But like wild dogs thirsting for blood they continued on the warpath. Not one insulted or threatened her. She wondered, "Will these drunken Indians attack and destroy my dear ones in the car?"

During all this tumult, Lillian felt a sense of peace by repeating in her mind the scripture: "Thou wilt keep him in perfect peace, whose mind is stayed on thee: because he trusteth in thee" (Isaiah 26:3).

Then she heard shots and saw the Indians retreat before 250 soldiers. Fleeing for their lives in every direction, she saw them mowed down by gunfire. Soon the battle ceased, the soldiers cleared the road, and she heard the welcome sound of the Model T Ford chugging up the hill. That night, even though soldiers stayed around the mission, Indians slipped in to carry away their dead. When they couldn't remove some of the bodies, they disfigured their faces so they wouldn't be recognized.

After the trouble had died down and friendly Indians returned, they asked, "Why do you still keep soldiers around your house? We've seen as many as 300 at one time."

"Those aren't Ecuadorian soldiers," Orley answered. "Our God, who loves us, has sent His angel guard to protect us."

For eight years, Orley and Lillian had lived on the Andean continental divide of South America. Often they traveled west to the Pacific Ocean only 150 miles away. But what lay east and north along the rivers that flowed into the mighty Amazon and on to the Atlantic Ocean 3,500 miles away?

"Lillian, when we go home for furlough, would you be willing to endure the long, dangerous trip through the Amazon basin? We'd be completely dependent on Indian guides and carriers. Jungle travel means braving rapids and whirlpools, constant rain, and biting insects. Should we expose our children to the diseases found in the tropics?" Orley asked.

Lillian smiled. "Orley, nothing could be much worse than what we've gone through together in this so-called civilized part of Ecuador. Isn't God's power as great in the jungle as in the mountains?"

Orley hugged her tightly. "You're a real helpmate, my dear. No wonder I love you so much. You thrive on adventure too. But that's not my real reason for wanting to explore this little-known part of Ecuador."

"I know. You want to understand how to penetrate the many heathen villages that have never yet heard the gospel story. About how long would the trip take?"

"My guess is between two and three months, depending on delays waiting for carriers and guides who have no concept of time. Our furlough is due near the end of this year [1929], and the missionaries who will take our place will soon be here. How soon shall we start making preparations?" Orley asked.

"Why not begin now?" Lillian said, with a twinkle in her eyes.

"Am I glad I married a NOW girl!" Orley picked her up and started for the door, laughing. "Mrs. Ford, you are on your way!"

"Hold it!" she squealed. "There are four of us, you know."

Busy days of packing, selling, turning things over to the new missionaries, and saying goodbye to faithful friends and patients came to an end on November 21, 1929. By car they wound down the mountainous road ninety miles to Baños, the last bit of civilization before they plunged into the jungle.

On muleback, led by two Indian boys, they followed the Pastaza River along a narrow trail where one foot dangled in space and the other often scraped against a rock wall. Two-year-old Sylvia rode with Daddy, but eight-year-old Elden felt very grown up on his own Indian pony.

Forty miles of traveling without seeing a single inhabited spot brought them to Mera, a cluster of palm-thatched huts. This settlement, one of the world's wettest spots, was the gateway to the trackless forest beyond.

"Here's where I arranged to meet our Indian guides," Orley explained, as they crowded into a room in one of the huts.

"I'm so glad for this shelter, with the rain pouring down outside," Lillian said, as she began to peel off the children's wet clothes. "The owner of this 'lodge' said this is the dry season. What would the wet season be like?"

For two weeks they waited for their guides, who had to travel from the distant Napo River. During this time they shared the gospel with their hosts, who eagerly listened and sometime later became baptized Christians.

"Look, Daddy." Elden pointed to twelve naked men filing silently out of the forest. "Here come our guides! Wow, do they look great painted with so many colors and designs!" Each carried a walking stick, a machete, and a woven fiber knapsack swung from his forehead down over his back. Since Elden spoke Quechua like a native, he soon made friends with them.

"They told me they'd been delayed getting their food ready," the little interpreter explained to his parents. "You'll never guess how they did it. Everybody chewed cassava root until it was soft, then spit it into banana leaves. They wrapped it into packages of several pounds each and hid them for use along the way back. I'm glad we have our own kind of food."

That evening the Fords packed everything into rubber bags. Early the next morning, their guides started through the dense jungle, swinging their machetes to the right and left to cut a trail. Struggling to keep up, Orley and Lillian stooped and squeezed through the openings cut for them. They steadied themselves with poles as they crossed fallen logs submerged in water or scrambled over the debris on the forest floor. Sylvia, and usually Elden, rode on chairs on the backs of the Indians. Sometimes when the mud became impassable or the river too deep, Lillian also rode along on the back of these strong, sure-footed guides.

Each night, the Indians built lean-tos of palm leaves, which kept out the downpours.

"I'm so tired, this cot seems better than an innerspring mattress," Orley said.

"I love the sounds of a jungle night. What a concert!" Lillian lay listening. "I can hear monkeys screaming, cougars crying, and wild pigs grunting, plus the calls of parrots and many other wild creatures. What could be more thrilling than this— a black jungle night, surrounded by savage Indians, wild animals, and snakes . . ."

"And don't forget our angels, Mother," Elden added.

For six days they tramped through the deep forest, marveling at the luxuriant plants, trees, brilliant orchids, and butterflies, such a contrast from the bleak highlands of the last eight years.

"We're here," Orley shouted joyously. "From now on it's the great waterways that lead to the Amazon. We've completed the difficult journey by land. Next come the thrills and fears of riding at breakneck speed in Indian canoes."

Even little Sylvia learned to sit very still in the twenty-foot-long, three-foot-wide, hollowed-out tree trunk, so skillfully guided by canoemen who shot rapids and dodged boulders and whirlpools in the treacherous rivers.

"I'm so glad when we stop on the sandbars," Elden said, as he watched the Indians build fires from the driftwood and then hurry off to fish. "Let's catch more fireflies, Sylvia, so we can play toy cars." He put several insects on cane stalks. "Look, their headlights turn on high or dim, and they have tiny green taillights too."

Gradually the rivers became wider and less swift. A new canoe, forty feet long, with a palm-leaf canopy to protect them from the sun and rain, gave Lillian an opportunity to resume Elden's second-grade classwork. Often they interrupted arithmetic and reading with, "See that giant tree with the huge buttress." "Look at the huge hornbill perched on that limb." "There's a tapir feeding along the riverbank."

Often they changed guides and canoemen and spent many days waiting at jungle outposts for the new ones.

ADVENTURES GALORE! 41

Fierce, savage Indian tribes lived along the Napo River. For several hundred miles, they kept the big canoe as far from their side of the river as possible, knowing that many travelers had been killed by their blowguns.

Once, a canoe from these hostile Indians came alongside their large one, and Elden, speaking Quechua, told them they were missionaries.

"I wish you would come and teach my people," one Indian said.

Pastor Ford, holding the two canoes together, prayed with them. As they drifted apart, he said, "Even in their ignorance, these people are searching for something better. If only God will open the way to reach them."

After traveling for fifty-two days, they reached Iquitos, where they received a cordial welcome from Pastor and Mrs. F. A. Stahl. What a joy to wear dry clothes, bathe and dress in privacy, and eat at a table. While they waited for the monthly riverboat that would take them north to the mouth of the Amazon, the two pioneer missionary families shared many precious visits.

"Now you've seen the challenge of taking the gospel to the many people who live along the rivers that flow into the Amazon," said Pastor Stahl.

"True, I've caught a vision on this trip I'll never forget."

Fourteen more days on the riverboat brought them to Belem, Brazil.

As they walked up the gangplank of the steamship bound for New York, Orley said, "I feel so grateful to God for His love and care over us on this eighty-three-day journey across South America's wildest forests."

"But I do have some concerns about our arrival in the U.S.," Lillian added. "What will people think when we step off the ship in the cold of winter dressed in summer clothes with five monkeys, two lovebirds, and a parrot?"

"I just hope they'll admit us into the country." Orley laughed.

Chapter 8
Guatemala for God

Passengers smiled as little Sylvia roamed the ship's deck, hugging her tame monkey, its woolly arms circling her neck. Gradually they left the warmth of the tropics. Cold March winds blew across the water.

One chilly night, Orley awoke, saying, "I'm afraid those monkeys may be cold down in the hold of the ship. Maybe I'd better bring them to our warm cabin."

Feeling his way across the dark deck, he stumbled over a ventilator, fell, and hit his nose. Blood spurted out. After examination, the ship's doctor declared, "I'm sorry, Mr. Ford, but your nose is broken. You'll need to wear a bandage for some time."

They brought their pets to the cabin, but Sylvia's tame monkey died despite their best efforts.

The morning they entered New York Harbor, Orley announced, "Guess what? We're landing in a March blizzard."

"At least you'll be color-coordinated in your white suit, straw hat, and big white bandage." Lillian smiled. "Any suggestions on how we can keep the monkeys, birds, and us from freezing while we wait for a taxi to take us to the hotel?"

Orley thought a while. "Only one, but you won't like it. Remember the Indian blankets we bought to give away to friends? There are enough in the trunk to cover the monkey crates and bird cages and wrap around each of us."

Lillian groaned. "What a choice! Catch cold or provide amusement for the citizens of New York! All right, get the blankets."

The next morning, wrapped in blankets, the family went shopping for winter clothes. When Lillian entered the dress shop, she folded the blanket over one arm and explained to the friendly clerk, "We just arrived from the tropics and have no winter apparel. I'd like a blue suit with matching accessories."

Clothed in her new purchases, she stood before the full length mirror. "You don't look like the same lady," the clerk exclaimed.

Taking the train to Detroit, the family took delivery of a new Ford car at the factory.

"Do I ever like the smooth paved roads, Daddy!" little Elden said. "And the yummy food at the restaurants!"

"And the clean potties," added little Sylvia.

"I appreciate the motels," Lillian added. Turning to Orley, she asked, "Are you wondering what God has planned for our future?"

"You may be sure that if we trust Him for guidance, He has something better." He smiled.

The Fords distributed the monkeys and birds to relatives along the way to Loma Linda. During their furlough, Elden enjoyed third grade in his first American school.

The "something better" proved to be a big change from Peru and Ecuador. Called to the springlike climate of Guatemala in 1931, Orley faced a new challenge as mission president.

Soon after the family arrived in Guatemala City, Orley told Lillian, "I've discovered we have only twenty-five Adventist Christians in this big Catholic city. I've rented a large theater downtown for meetings. Now I need to practice my Spanish. I think I'll go down into that deep ravine near our house, where I can talk out loud and not disturb anyone."

But when Lillian heard her frightened neighbor exclaim, "There's a crazy man down there waving his arms around and raving!" she decided to convince her preacher to prepare his sermons at home.

On the opening night, 1,000 people crowded the hall, some pushing so hard to get in that they broke the glass on the doors. But on the third night, they found twelve policemen standing guard and the doors locked.

"What's the trouble?" Ford asked.

"You've broken the law! You can't hold religious meetings in a public building, only in your own church."

In desperation, Ford sought the advice of the American consul.

"Don't you know there's a law against holding Protestant meetings in the middle of a Catholic city?" he said. "Find some small place at the edge of town."

Hearing of the trouble, the minister of public works, a friend of Ford's, came up with an idea. "Yes, you're now breaking the law, but put up a large sign with the words, 'Templo Adventista' on the theater, and if anyone objects, tell them this: 'We rented the hall; now it's our church, and we have a right to preach in our own temple.'"

Orley had the sign made. Then his friend went with him to see the minister of education. "Mr. Ford has had a little trouble. The police closed his church, so he can't have religious services," he said.

"Oh," he said, "I thought he was having meetings in a public hall."

"Send an inspector to check and see. You'll find they're being held in the 'Templo Adventista.'"

That ended the trouble. With God's blessing, those three months of meetings ended with forty members added to the Adventist Church.

Soon a church school with thirty pupils opened with Lillian serving as Bible and music teacher. When Elden finished the six grades at the church school, he continued studying by correspondence. Because he wanted to be with the other boys and girls, he rode his bicycle twenty-two blocks to the church school to do his studying.

Another joy came to the family when little brown-eyed Donnie was born. How Elden and Sylvia adored their new baby brother!

Often they took him out into the large yard surrounding their home. He laughed as they played games with the young people from the church, or he watched them do their chores—caring for the garden, the cow, rabbits, chickens, and bees.

One evening when Daddy came home, he found Lillian and the children playing with their pet monkey. Sitting down on the grass with them, he said, "Lillian, we need someone to direct the Sabbath School and Missionary Volunteer activities for the Guatemala mission. Because you love young people so much, would you consider accepting a new challenge?"

"But I don't want to be away from our children."

"You don't have to go to the mission office. You can set up a desk at home, write letters, and send out materials from here. Then the whole family can visit country churches while we help organize Sabbath Schools and youth societies."

And that's just what they did.

A year later, the Ford family rushed around the house getting everything ready for the many guests who would be coming for the year-end mission business meetings.

Busy planning menus, Lillian said to Elden, "I'm so glad we have our own cow so I can make fresh cottage cheese. By the way, she's full of ticks. Could you go to the drugstore and get some medicine for her?"

Elden applied it carefully to the cow's tick-infested hide. Unfortunately, no one warned him to tie her head so she couldn't lick the medicine. The next morning, they found her dead.

Constantly Orley and Lillian carried in their hearts the desire to bring the good news of salvation to the entire country of Guatemala. That's why Orley chose to go on long trips, sometimes up to three months. They battled with loneliness; Lillian, caring for the children and her church work in the city, and Orley, missing his beloved family.

"I must visit the country's Indians who live in the crowded communities of the western highlands," he said with conviction. "These colorful tribes—pagans and spirit worshipers at heart—still cling to their old ways. Yet I know that when they experience the power of Jesus' love, many will become firm and loyal Christians."

And so it happened. However, the gospel message had not yet reached the northern plains section of El Petén.

"Lillian, I've heard of interested persons in the Petén region. I must go and seek them out," he said.

"But you can only go a short distance by car. There are no roads," she objected.

"I still have two good legs," he countered. "I'm sure I can get Alfred Lutz to go with me. We'll hire a couple of Indians to carry our baggage and food. There's occasional plane service to Flores, so you can write to me. I'll send a letter of our progress to you from there.

"Anyway, this is the dry season. In that vast jungle, the springs overflow during the rainy season but are completely dry now." Orley smiled at his wife, who still looked concerned.

"My dear," Orley said, hugging Lillian. "You do care a lot for me, don't you? Let's put our trust in Jesus and claim God's promise in Isaiah 33:16, 'Bread shall be given him; his waters shall be sure.' "

After the last bumpy road petered out, the two men set out on foot, sleeping at night on the ground. True to Lillian's fears, they often searched desperately for wells or springs of water. Lutz became so thirsty, he began having hallucinations. When they finally found a muddy pool, Orley, also parched with thirst, knelt down and drank the filthy liquid, unmindful of the consequences. Fortunately, he vomited it up.

They came upon ancient Mayan cities matted with the growth of centuries, silent cities with fallen images and crumbling pyramids and towers. For many days they walked without seeing a single human being.

After two weeks of extremely difficult travel, they came to the town of Flores and the large lake in the midst of the Petén. "Let's hire a dugout canoe, cross the lake, and wait for the mail plane from Guatemala City. Maybe there's news from home," Orley suggested.

They boarded and told a woman on shore, "Give us a shove."

She did, but with so much vigor that the boat capsized. But such minor problems as a good soaking didn't daunt the travelers, who continued eastward to the coast of the Caribbean Sea. Their six-weeks' walk of 300 miles ended in Belize. Thus began a work for God in Central America that continues to grow.

When Orley came home, Lillian shared the news. "Orley, wonderful word has come. So many Indians have accepted Christ that they need to build a larger church at Mazatenango. But they're too poor, and few can read or write."

"Do you have any suggestions of what we can do?" he asked.

"Well, we've been saving for a different car. You know how these roads have beat up our old Ford. Sometimes I fear it won't make it to church. I've been skimping in every way I could, and I think we have around $300."

"Good girl! You're a real missionary wife!" Orley smiled. "Are you suggesting that you and the children join me on another walking trip for our coming furlough to the U.S.?"

"Oh, Orley!" she said. "Haven't you heard of God's promises? Let's help build the church and trust Him when He says, 'My God shall supply all your needs.' I can hardly wait to see what a bargain He has for us."

When furlough time came, the family took the train to Mexico City. Orley began car shopping, but the secondhand ones cost between $500 and $600. He came back disappointed.

"Why don't you drop in at the American consul's office? Maybe he can give you some ideas on purchasing a car," Lillian suggested.

After Orley explained his problem, the friendly official said, "We have an old car behind the house. The American who owned it died, and we must get the car back to the U.S."

Orley inspected the three-year-old Chevrolet.

"It seems as if it's in good condition, but should a Ford buy a Chevy?"

"How much can you pay?" asked the consul.

"I have $100," stated the missionary.

"We dare not let it go that cheap! Yet we need to get rid of it." He thought a while. "I think I'll give you a real bargain. You can have it for $115."

Though Orley felt a little disloyal not staying with Fords, he bought the car. They drove it over 10,000 miles on roads in Mexico and the U.S. without any trouble. And God proved His promises of adding "much more" when Orley sold it—for $250!

Chapter 9
Their Ultimate Sacrifice

Sacrifices had become such a way of life for the Fords that they seldom recognized them as such. Yet now they faced a heartbreaking decision.

"Son," Orley said to Elden, "the time has come for us to return to Guatemala. You're now 15 and enjoying your schoolwork at San Diego Academy. Shall Mother and I leave you here to study and associate with the young people of your own country? Or do you want to return with us? We hate to go back without you."

"Guatemala's my home, Dad, and my closest friends live there. But I'll admit I enjoy studying with other students rather than taking correspondence alone. Could I spend my summer vacations with you?"

"Of course you may. We'll work out some way to pay for your travel."

After much prayer and tears, the Fords sailed out of San Diego Harbor with Elden waving from the dock. Nine-year-old Sylvia cried, but little Donnie's heart-rending call, "Daddy, Daddy, stop the ship. They're leaving Elden behind," almost broke the parents' hearts. Elden had always taken care of Donnie, and the little three-year-old boy knew something was terribly wrong.

A year later, Elden traveled by second-class train through Mexico and reached home for only $25. That summer, he worked selling Spanish books in Guatemala. Jubilant to have his big brother with the family again, Donnie objected strenuously when he returned to school in the U.S. at the end of the summer.

The Fords spent eleven years in Guatemala. When they returned for their next furlough in 1942, Elden, a college student of twenty-one, introduced them to his special girlfriend, Venessa.

"Are you ready for a new challenge?" Orley asked Lillian.

"What next?"

"Why, something better, of course," he teased.

"What could be better than Guatemala?"

"We've been asked to go south to Costa Rica, another small, mountainous country. Though it's just northwest of Panama, San José, the capital, enjoys an ideal daytime temperature of 75 to 80 degrees year-round. You'll like the fertile farming lands and beautiful forests in this progressive, modern country."

As president of the Costa Rica Mission, Orley soon encountered opposition from a populace that was 90 percent Catholic. During an evangelistic meeting in San José, a large group of boys and girls on the street began making all kinds of noise in front of the door. When Orley stepped out in the darkness, they could see him, but he couldn't see them.

Waving his arms, he called out, "Please go away and be quiet."

They ran all directions. Some tumbled into a ditch as they fled. As Orley returned to the hall, he heard the cry of a little girl.

Sometime later, the police came to the hall saying, "Please report to headquarters." Thinking it might be some trouble between church members, Orley dismissed it as of little importance and didn't go until the following morning.

He sat for some time, waiting for the officer to come to him. Suddenly, he felt a terrific blow to his head. His glasses flew across the room. Blood spurted from his nose and eyes. The policemen rushed in and restrained the man who had attacked Orley from behind. He was the father of the little girl who had fallen into the ditch the night before.

Hardly able to talk, Orley tried to explain he had neither

seen nor touched the child. They released him, but he had difficulty making his way to the doctor.

"One of your eyes is so badly injured, I fear you may lose the sight in it," he said after examination.

A short time later, a lawyer called, "Mr. Ford, I'm calling on behalf of the man who attacked you. How much will you take to drop the case?"

"Sir," Ford answered, "I do not plan to take this matter to court. I leave all such dealings with God."

Filled with gratitude, the Fords praised God when the eye healed. They also felt grateful that Sylvia could attend the Costa Rica training school only a few miles from home. Here, she lived in the dormitory and studied in Spanish with young people from all over Central America. Only one other American student, also from a missionary family, attended. Sylvia and Marvin Larson became special friends.

Donnie, however, kept the home lively. If his parents had permitted him to do so, he would have taken in every stray dog and cat. Donnie treated his own dog as if he were human. They shared a deep, unselfish relationship, as he spent the best of his life with his pet. Not only did he love animals, but everything about nature also intrigued him. He thrilled with each new discovery.

"Mother, please come quickly," Donnie often called. "Let's watch Jesus paint the sunset." Hand in hand, they would marvel at the beauty of the clouds.

"I found a new flower, Mother. Please come and tell me what it is." Donnie's life filled their home with delight, discovery, beauty, and joy.

Mother and son often shopped together at the local market. Lillian knew how to spread her table with the delicious foods grown in the country, instead of buying expensive imported food from a tin can. She enjoyed a few modern conveniences in her Costa Rica home. No longer did she have to make furniture from boxes and dress them up with pretty material. For the first time, she had a few luxuries common in the U.S.

Every time Orley started meetings, nine-year-old Donnie got excited.

"Please, Dad. Let me run the projector for you. And I'd like to greet the people when they come in, too." He won more friends for the church with his smiles and cheery words than any preacher could. Whenever errands needed to be run, he spoke up quickly, "Sure, I'll go."

One morning, Orley said to his boy, "Donnie, I'm going to be gone for a few days. We've had wonderful news. Thirty-six people have given their hearts to Jesus and are waiting for baptism. So I have the joy of preaching the sermon and then baptizing them. I wish you could go with me."

"I do, too, Daddy, but I don't feel very good. Mother says I've been running a little fever. I don't think she'll let me go."

"It's probably better that you get over this bug first. Let's plan on your going with me on my next trip. OK?" Orley ruffled his son's hair and gave him an affectionate hug. "See you in a few days," he called as he went out the door.

Donnie's slight fever continued. His dog stayed by his side.

"You'd better stay in bed today, Donnie," Lillian said.

"But I need to feed my dog. You know he has to eat three times a day."

"I'll make a deal with you. If you'll stay quiet and drink lots of water, I'll feed your dog three times today."

That evening, Lillian spent a longer than usual bedtime hour reading stories with Donnie.

"I like it when we have such a long, special time together," he said as she kissed him goodnight. His forehead felt hotter than it had a few hours before.

Concerned, she checked on him often through the night. Watching his restless sleep, she remembered how often their special times together had been cut short because of mission responsibilities. Was leading out in Missionary Volunteer youth work, helping in the Dorcas Society, or answering letters more important? she wondered.

"Oh, God," she prayed, "help me to realize that my greatest mission field is my own precious boy. And give me wisdom to make the right choices. I need You to help me care for him now."

But the next morning, Donnie felt worse. His fever rose

rapidly, but he remembered to ask, "Mother, did you feed my dog?"

Within a few hours, Donnie died.

Immediately, she sent word to Orley. He received the message just as he entered the pulpit. Since he was the only ordained minister present and thirty-six people awaited baptism, he went ahead, though his heart was breaking. Trusting in His Father's sustaining grace, Orley somehow got through the service. Oh, how he longed to go home, but he had no way to leave town until the next morning.

As the grieving couple stood amid Costa Rica's tropical greenery by Donnie's grave, their minds turned to baby Teddy's grave on the barren Andes in Peru and to little Arlis's grave on the plains of Kansas, and they pleaded, "Come quickly, Lord Jesus."

For a time, the brokenhearted missionaries could not continue their work. They needed to get away to rest and think. They chose a little village by the sea, where, surrounded by the beauty of the nature Donnie loved, they could experience healing.

Walking down the streets overgrown with grass, they made their way under the coconut palms to a knoll where a little Adventist church stood. There, in that quiet place, they began to find the peace and courage to go on.

"God lent us our boy for nine years, years of happiness for him and for us. He was the sunlight of our home, and now he's gone," Lillian sobbed. "I can't understand why God in His infinite love and wisdom has permitted us to be separated."

"But nothing can dim the sweet memories; memories of love that we will recount over and over again," Orley added. "Right now, it seems that our work will be crippled without Donnie."

"Wouldn't Donnie have loved it here?" Lillian spread her arms, pointing as she spoke. "Look at the fruit trees he enjoyed—breadfruit, custard-apple, papaya, orange, lime, and avocado. What fun he would have had, picking, tasting, and sharing them all."

They sat quietly holding hands, letting the tears fall. "Somehow God will help us to pull together the tangled threads again." Orley stopped, too choked up to speak. Finally, he added, "Only His grace can enable us to submit humbly to our loss. Someday we'll understand our Father's will."

Yet even as they grieved, the Fords reached out to others. Every night Orley held meetings in the little church. The isolated believers attended with grateful hearts. And Lillian, putting aside her grief, turned to the children, holding special classes in nature and self-improvement. Before they left, the Fords conducted an investiture service for twenty, both young people and those not so young. One man eighty years old proudly received his "Friend" pin.

When they returned home, they continued on in their service for God, though everything, everywhere reminded them of Donnie. God blessed their efforts, as they combined medical missionary work with evangelistic efforts. Even in this conservative country, in a seven-week series of meetings, they had to hold two services each evening to accommodate the crowds. Why? Because Orley extracted nearly 2,000 teeth, offering free dental services to those needing help.

Another blessing came into their lives. A year after Donnie's death in 1943, Elden and his talented young bride, Venessa, arrived as missionaries in Central America. First, they visited Orley and Lillian and then went on to Honduras to open a ten-grade school in the Bay Islands.

In 1945, the Fords returned to the U.S. for another furlough. Sylvia, still with them, spent part of her academy school year in Washington, D.C., and the rest in California. While the Fords were there, friends came to them, suggesting, "We know of someone who might help heal the hurt of Donnie's death. We don't think it's a coincidence that a little three-year-old boy with the surname of Ford needs a home. Would you go see him?"

The moment Orley and Lillian saw his brown eyes, so like Donnie's, they fell in love with little Billy. Yes, they would take him as God's gift of love to help heal their home and hearts.

Chapter 10
Living on Promise

Orley strode into the house at his usual fast pace.

"Where are you, Lillian?" he called. Urgency filled his voice.

"Right here," she answered, as she hurried toward him. "Is something wrong?"

"No, but God's done it again."

"Done what?"

"I've just been appointed president of the El Salvador Mission. Do you suppose God is offering us 'something better' again?"

"I'm sure He is. He gave us fifteen years in South America, eleven years in Guatemala, three and a half in Costa Rica, and now we're called to the smallest of Central America's countries."

"But only in area, not people," Orley added. "Did you know the population density is almost as much as India's? The masses struggle in poverty, tilling all available land, almost to the top of the steep slopes of the volcanoes."

"There's one sure fact. I love the name of the country, which in Spanish means 'The Saviour,'" Lillian said, smiling. "Wherever He calls, I'm ready to go."

"Then you'll like the capital city even better, for it's called San Salvador, meaning 'Holy Saviour of the World.' With 80 percent of all Salvadorans Roman Catholic, and only 3 percent Protestants, we surely need our Saviour's help," Orley added.

And they did! Though they loved their new country, the moderate climate, and their home encircled by mountains, problems continually arose which involved the Fords. The contrast between the well-to-do landowners and the destitute poor created tension, political unrest, and suspicion. People were arrested on the slightest pretext.

One day, Orley received the message, "I'm in prison. Please come and help me." The note was signed by a young literature evangelist.

Working near the Salvador-Honduras border, the young man had sent a telegram ordering more books and magazines. In order to save money, he had given only the number and first word of the titles. His telegram read, "I urgently need 7 Enough, 4 Victories, 8 Horizons, 7 Times, 20 Nurses, 20 Watchman."

Police intercepted the suspicious telegram, sending it to the president of the country. Intelligence agents decided that the Spanish word for *enough* looked like bazooka, a portable rocket launcher. They thought *horizons* referred to some instrument for observation, *times* meant time bombs, and *nurses* and *watchmen* referred to soldiers.

Pastor Ford explained the message carefully to the police, who promptly freed the young man.

Frequent crosses marked the roadsides, indicating violence and death. One three-mile stretch in front of a small Seventh-day Adventist church had seven crosses, all scenes of assassinations. One evening, as Orley walked toward the church thinking of the sadness and hurt these crosses meant, he heard a wild yell.

Glancing behind him, he saw a drunk racing toward him armed with a large knife. Orley, who kept himself in top physical condition, used his long legs to outrun the criminal. He vaulted over an adobe wall and hid in a hut. People nearby heard the commotion, overpowered the drunk, and tied him up, while Pastor Ford rejoiced in the promise, "To God, the Lord, belongs escape from death" (Psalm 68:20, RSV).

A young minister named David helped Orley hold meetings in Santa Ana, the second largest city in El Salvador.

"Pastor Ford," he said. "I fear the local priest is planning trouble. During Holy Week, the 'faithful' have been called to take part in a special procession. They will carry the virgin through the streets, imploring her to drive out the heretics. In response to their petitions, they plan to stone us."

"Time to pray, David, and claim my favorite promise, 'God is our refuge and strength, a very present help in trouble' (Psalm 46:1). But we need to do our part, too, so I'm going to ask for a number of plainclothes policemen to guard our hall during the meetings," Ford answered.

That night, someone tossed a flaming, kerosene-soaked broom through an open window where the choir sat. Everyone jumped away, except one woman, who quickly smothered the flames with her clothes and stamped on the broom. Outside, thousands of people carrying the virgin image stopped at the cross street just before the hall, blocked by parked trucks and armed police. Frustrated, they turned away, the meetings continued, and David and Orley praised God.

Not always did the police cooperate with Pastor Ford. One young man, whom the Fords had helped with school expenses, turned from God, mistreated his family, and became involved in plans to overthrow the government, while pretending to be a Christian. One evening Ford answered a knock on his door. A little child handed him a note from the traitor's wife.

"Mamma's hiding. Please help her," the youngster said.

The note explained, "My husband's away on a trip. I've sold everything and need to have my money changed into dollars so I can leave the country before he returns. Could you help me get a bank draft?"

Ford found her in a miserable hut. Learning the details, Ford realized she needed to flee and secured the bank draft.

The next Sabbath, two plainclothes policemen appeared at church and summoned Orley to headquarters.

"I can't go now," he said. "I'm very busy today."

"We'll wait," they replied. "It will take only a few minutes."

"If you promise I can come right back, I'll go with you."

They promised, so he left without telling anyone.

But at the police station, all seemed different. Taking his wallet and belt, they said, "You're under arrest."

"May I phone my wife?"

LIVING ON PROMISE 57

"No, prisoners aren't allowed to phone."

Glancing around, he saw a friendly policeman he knew and called to him.

"You keep out of this!" they warned. Grabbing a club, they shoved him into a cell with fifteen other men. Puzzled, Ford tried to figure out why he had been arrested. He didn't understand until noon, when the officer began questioning him.

"Where is the woman and her children?" they demanded.

"I don't know," he answered truthfully.

"If you do not tell us where she is hiding or where she fled, we'll torture you."

"I know nothing. I only helped her get a bank draft."

In desperation, the officer finally pushed him into a filthy cell, crammed with unkempt criminals lying on the slimy floor. He saw no furniture in the room but an open latrine and a faucet. Still dressed in his white suit, Orley felt strangely out of place. Though weary, he hated to sit down and soil his good suit. Gratefully, he accepted the offer of two men who shared a torn piece of matting. Sitting there, he prayed, "God, you said, 'Call to Me, and I will answer you, and show you great and mighty things, which you do not know'" (Jeremiah 33:3, NKJV).

Late that afternoon, handcuffed and chained to a guard, he was escorted down the street by seven policemen.

"We're going to search your house," they stated.

Several church members saw them go by and ran to see their pastor.

"Better watch out for me; I'm a dangerous criminal." Ford laughed as he spoke. But he really worried that his pants would fall down since he had no belt and was handcuffed.

They made him and his guard sit on the patio while they ransacked his house. He knew they'd need much time, for all the books, notebooks, and photograph albums were in English. A crowd gathered, but soon, two men pushed through.

"Look here; you can't do this to our neighbor," they threatened the policeman. "Mr. Ford's our friend, and we demand you release him." In anger, they abruptly left.

Twenty minutes later, another policemen arrived and ordered, "Take those handcuffs off. Two lawyers just telephoned the president of the republic, who requests the release of the prisoner. Here are your belt and billfold, Mr. Ford."

God's great and mighty things were those two men, whom Ford had never met. They not only demanded his freedom, but insisted on an editorial in the paper, apologizing for the event.

Though president of the mission, Ford never lost his love for the simple people. Often, he went to out-of-the-way places where no car could travel and he needed a horse. While passing through a small town, a woman stopped him.

"You pastor that pulls teeth?" she asked.

"Yes I am." He nodded. His dental services had not ended with the Indians of Ecuador.

"Hurt bad." She pointed into her mouth.

He took his dental instruments from his saddlebag, set the patient on a chair in her yard, and removed the offending tooth. A crowd quickly gathered, and before he could mount his horse again, he had pulled twenty-five teeth.

"Please stay. Others need help too," they begged.

"But I have a meeting tonight in a town farther up the mountain."

"Why don't you stay here and have a meeting? We'd all like to come."

"But you folks have threatened to stone any Protestant who came here," he objected.

"Oh, but not you. We'll protect you. You may have the meeting at our home," several offered.

Another spoke up, "I can arrange for the schoolhouse."

That night, 200 people came to listen to the gospel story. Pastor Ford's medical missionary work opened another door.

Returning from a trip of visiting churches near the Guatemalan border, Ford had another opportunity to trust God's promises in a time of crisis. Recent political disturbances made the police suspicious of all foreigners. At a junction, a policeman boarded the train and asked him for his identification papers.

Reaching into all his pockets, Ford shook his head. "I'm sorry, sir. I neglected to take them with me on this short trip.

I haven't left the country. My name is Orley Ford, I live in San Salvador, and I will be happy to have you call my office or home."

"Get off the train at once!" the policeman ordered, pushing a gun against Ford's ribs.

Another policeman appeared with handcuffs, locked them on Ford's wrists, and told him to sit on a bench near the station. For one hour, Ford sat in the cold rain, waiting for the policemen to finish their drinks.

"We have orders to march you to Santa Ana fifteen miles away. Get up and get going!" they demanded.

"You have my wallet. Please take the money from it and hire a car, and we'll ride together. I have this heavy suitcase filled with books, clothes, and my dental equipment, you know," Ford suggested.

"No, prisoners have to walk. The suitcase is your problem," the half-drunk policemen replied.

A lady standing nearby, who had heard everything, spoke up, "Please, let me take care of it for you. Where shall I deliver it?"

Ford wondered, Should I trust this stranger? But he had no choice. "Better take it to the jail," he answered.

The strange trio started out, the tall, gray-haired prisoner in the lead, followed by the policemen. Going uphill most of the way, Orley walked vigorously to get warm. As he walked, he repeated promises, "Fear not, for I am with you; be not dismayed, for I am your God. I will strengthen you, yes, I will help you, I will uphold you with My righteous right hand" (Isaiah 41:10, NKJV).

Puffing and panting, his captors couldn't keep up. They called ahead,

"Please go slower. There's no hurry."

With his usual sense of humor, Orley called back, "It's getting dark and raining. Surely you young fellows can keep up with this old gray-haired man." And he lengthened his stride.

"Please, please go slower. We can't walk that fast."

"That's strange. I was the one who wanted to take the car. You fellows wanted to walk." Orley grinned to himself as he walked vigorously thirty feet ahead of them. Occasionally, he called back, "Better watch out. This dangerous criminal might get away from you."

But as they neared Santa Ana, he slowed down, sang gospel songs and told his captors about his work and his beloved Jesus. They arrived at one o'clock in the morning, when Orley lay down to sleep on the cold cement in the open patio of the prison.

When the offices opened at 8:00 a.m., Orley requested that a telegram be sent for him to the governor of the state, a friend of his. Some time later, the governor appeared, exclaiming, "What are you doing here, Mr. Ford?" Then turning to the policemen, he ordered, "Take those handcuffs off, give him his wallet, and arrange for him to return to San Salvador."

Just then, an old lady came trudging along with a heavy suitcase on her back.

"Please, let me pay you for all your trouble," Orley exclaimed in gratitude.

"No, sir." She smiled. "I came to the city on a truck, and I was glad to carry it the mile from the truck stop for you."

But she was delighted when the missionary visited her home in Santa Ana a short time later and presented her with a beautiful shawl.

Five years passed. "I'm so glad our furlough comes at Sylvia's graduation time from Union College," Lillian said. "And that the romance begun at the training school in Costa Rica will give us another son. With Marvin finishing ministerial training and Sylvia, nurse's training, they should be a great team for God."

"May we go to her wedding and then to California for Elden's graduation too?" Billy interrupted.

Two years later, Marvin and Sylvia Larson joined the college staff in Costa Rica. Later they helped to build and run a new hospital in Nicaragua. Elden and his family returned to the Bay Islands in Honduras.

"How God has blessed!" Lillian exclaimed. "Could any greater joy come to us than to have our children devote their lives to the missions we love?"

Chapter 11
Challenges Never Cease

Back in El Salvador, the Fords struggled to carry on God's work with inadequate help. The mission could afford to employ only four ordained ministers. Some of the dedicated national workers cared for as many as twenty churches and groups. Despite the lack of leaders, the simple, loyal church members allowed the Holy Spirit to use them, and the gospel message made progress. But not without problems.

In one village, an active member received this message: "Stop your preaching, or you will be killed."

He kept right on. One evening at dusk, he and his eighteen-year-old son were riding home on horseback when two men, hired criminals, stepped from behind the trees fifty yards away and began firing guns. From the opposite side, another bandit began to shoot. Instantly, the man and his son slid from their saddles, dropped to the ground, and rolled into some bushes.

Feeling sure they had accomplished their job, the hired criminals rode away to get their money.

"They're gone," the father whispered.

"And look, Dad, the ground is strewed with empty shells. How could those experienced gunmen have such poor aim? I'm going to pick them up to see how many shots were fired."

He picked up forty-three empty shells. When they arrived home, his wife met him. "Are you all right? I've had such a strong impression that you were in danger, so I've been praying earnestly for your safety."

"Thank you, my dear," her husband said. "Only the power of God saved us. Just look at these many empty shells all meant to end our lives."

In another area, Juan Paul Perla lived up to his name, a genuine pearl for Christ. When he met Jesus, he was an unlearned, barefoot farmer. At first his neighbors threatened his life, and ran him out of town. Fighting discouragement, he resolved, "I have many brothers and sisters that I want with me in heaven. If I don't share God's love with them and my friends, how will they know?"

Five years later, he told Pastor Ford, "Today, thirty-two of my own family, all Pearls, have given their hearts to God. We have a total of three new Sabbath Schools and fifty new church members. But I must win more for God!"

Fifteen years later, Juan Perla was the recognized "father" of five churches with more than fifty members each. Because he paid a faithful tithe, God had blessed him financially, too, for now he owned the best store in town, his own home, and a large new truck to carry on his business.

Another dedicated member, Alberto, sent the Fords a letter. "My employer and many others want to hear more of Jesus. Please come to Poloros and help me."

"You mean we must drive over that tortuous road again? Do you think we can make it?"

Orley laughed. "Haven't you heard that people claim that the missionary's station wagon can even climb stairs?"

"It just about takes that on the road to Poloros," Lillian agreed.

They finally arrived in Poloros at dusk. Alberto had waited for them to explain, "My employer lives six miles from town. We must walk, for the road's impassable."

"But will the people wait that long for us?" Lillian asked.

"They'd wait all night just to hear you play your accordion."

Loaded with hammocks, flannelgraph, dental instruments, books, and the accordion, they made their way over the rough trail, arriving at nine o'clock. After many songs and a sermon, the Fords hung up their hammocks and soon fell asleep. Suddenly, they awakened at the sound of knocking.

CHALLENGES NEVER CEASE 63

"Please, won't you come and sing and preach once more? The villagers heard the music. Fifty people have gathered in the moonlight."

The tired missionaries didn't climb back into their hammocks until way after eleven o'clock. The next morning, a crowd had already gathered before they finished breakfast. Eagerly, the people listened as the Fords prayed, gave Bible studies, and visited the sick.

Before dawn the next morning, they awakened to singing, a bit off-key, but a love serenade to bid them goodbye.

"You don't need to go with us to the car, Alberto," Orley said. "You have work to do, and we can follow the trail. I can use this flashlight until it gets light."

In many places, the people had stacked poles across the trail to use as cattle guards to keep the animals out of the fields. Carefully Orley climbed over one of these rough stiles, handed Lillian the flashlight, stepped back—and disappeared.

"Orley, where are you?" Lillian called.

No answer.

Flashing her light, she saw a steep bank. Could he have fallen to the ravine below? Climbing up, she scanned the blackness with her light. Then she saw him wedged between a rock and some bushes. When she reached him, he gasped.

"I couldn't make a sound, for the pain was so intense. Guess that blow against the rock knocked out all my breath. I fear I've broken some ribs."

She helped him up the bank, and painfully he made his way to the car.

The rough road added to his pain. Back home the doctor confirmed the broken ribs, but Orley didn't slow down. Lillian had planned the first youth camp in Central America, and they needed to load supplies into their station wagon to take to the little schoolhouse near the coast.

"The boys can stay in one room, the girls in the other, and we'll use the long porch for crafts and classwork. We'll do fine with an open-air kitchen under the trees," Lillian explained. "We'll use the beach and woods for devotionals, games, campfires, hikes, and swimming."

Because Lillian wanted to get her hiking honor, she joined sixty other "young" people on an all-night twenty-two-mile hike in the rain and slept with them on the floor.

"Marvelous!" she exclaimed, as she looked across the rim of the enormous crater of the extinct volcano called Big Mouth.

Lillian loved to devote her time and energies to any project that involved young people. Could it have been because she missed her Donnie so much? She promoted children's Sabbath Schools, Adventist Youth honors and classes, Vacation Bible Schools, book clubs—all these and many more. Knowing that public schools insisted on Sabbath attendance, the Fords struggled to keep the little church schools open throughout the mission. They welcomed into their home many children from isolated country areas, who had no other opportunities to attend a church school.

For five or six years, Pastor Ford had been making plans for a new church. All this time, he had encouraged the members to save and plan and give. Now they had $10,000.

"I don't think the old building will hold out much longer. The pillars are so full of termites that I can insert my pocketknife the full length into the rotten wood," he told Lillian.

"And each week the rafters seem more bowed," she agreed. "But you haven't found a suitable building site."

"Right, and the buyer for the old church property told me that if I don't accept his offer by tomorrow, the deal is off. Time to pray and ask God to show us something better."

The next morning at six o'clock, the real estate agent rang their doorbell. "Could you come with me right away? I've found a lot I know you'll like."

Pastor Ford did like it. "Great! Good section of town, new buildings around it, and a ravine where the city plans to make a parkway along one side. How much is it?"

When he heard the price, Orley figured a while. Then he said, "The sale I have for the old property isn't quite enough."

"I have a friend who'll loan you the rest," the agent said.

The friend gladly loaned Pastor Ford the money, asked no interest, and didn't even request a guarantee.

"Now we can proceed," Orley told the building committee.

"But, Pastor, you've bought such a big piece of land in a far-out location, and your plans to construct a building that holds a thousand people seem too big," many criticized.

"We need room for a church school. Our membership will grow, and soon this will be in the heart of the official part of the city." Orley held out in faith. (Today, that church has to hold two services to accommodate its 2,000 members.)

The building contractor contacted Orley. "I think you should buy that piece of land across the street from this church we're building. I've noticed your house is in bad shape."

"You're right; it's about ready to fall down."

"I know you can get a good loan for building, and it will be easy to sell the old property," the contractor assured him.

Lillian agreed with Orley, so they, too, began to build. But when they moved into the new house, real estate values had gone down so much they couldn't sell the old house.

"Now we have two houses and a large debt. But I think the rent from the old house and the three apartments with it will be enough to keep up the payments, with a little left over. We can use that to send young people to our college in Costa Rica so they can become workers," he said.

That property didn't sell for ten years. God knew Orley needed that income. After he had paid his debts, he always had money to help worthy students and construct new churches.

"You're going to have a birthday soon, Orley," Lillian reminded him in December of 1958, "and this is your sixty-fifth."

"I've been thinking about this for some time now. Why don't we keep on working here without pay from the mission? That would allow El Salvador to take on an extra minister. I'm quite sure we could find something to do," and he winked at her.

As soon as he turned his office over to another, he accepted the responsibility for fourteen churches that had no pastor.

"At least they are all within a few miles of our home," he explained to Lillian. "Who knows, my dear? God's promises for our retirement might even offer something better than all these years before."

Chapter 12
The Greatest of These

All of those who knew the Fords felt that the location of their new home across the street from the new church was an advantage. The Fords sometimes wondered.

Many who thought of Orley and Lillian as father and mother used their home as a refuge. That included ministers, office workers, teachers, church members, rich and poor, young and old, yes, and even tourists. How did the Fords cope with the constant interruptions? Lillian and Orley had learned from their Friend, Jesus, that the greatest of men are those who serve. Never did they show any irritation but treated each guest with gracious kindness. From morning till night, the doorbell rang with endless requests. The girl who answered the door heard:

"May I borrow a hammer and a saw?

Would Mrs. Ford please write a program for Sabbath School?

I need an extension cord.

My mother is sick. Would the pastor please visit her?

Would Mrs. Ford have time to accompany me on this song?

Do you have any clothes for me and my children?

My daughter will soon be married. Could we have the reception here at the Ford's house?

Would Mrs. Ford please help me identify these insects for my MV honor?

The spirits are bothering my grandma. Will the pastor come and pray?

THE GREATEST OF THESE 67

I need to borrow money until next payday.

May I leave my little boy here for a few days while my wife has an operation?"

And each person went away feeling loved, knowing that the Fords cared about their needs.

"Papa and Mama Ford remind me of God. Like Him, they're always ready to help and willing to listen," said one young girl who lived in their home.

Another commented, "I've never heard Mrs. Ford raise her voice, nor have I seen any disagreement between husband and wife. They seem to understand each other so well that only a nod or a smile is necessary for communication between them."

Three years after Orley's retirement in 1961, a new worker arrived, so now the Fords had only six churches. "Since we have more time now, let's try to open up new work by starting an effort in the suburb of Villa Delgado on the far side of the city, about five miles away," Orley told Lillian.

This area had only small, government-built homes of just three or four little rooms. No halls could be rented.

"Since it's the dry season, let's rent an open lot, put up a six-foot board wall around it, erect a platform on one end, and begin open air meetings," Orley suggested.

"And who'll be on our evangelistic team?" Lillian asked.

"Simple." He smiled. "You'll be song director with your accordion. Then you can show a film on 'Adventures of the Bible,' and I'll give the sermon. We'll hold meetings five nights a week for three months and visit our churches over the weekends."

Between 100 and 200 attended each night. When the rains came, they closed the effort, but God had given them a good group of new believers.

"Now we must erect a church building, for it's too far to our central church. Remember that wealthy Catholic friend of mine who asked for help to overcome drinking and smoking?" Lillian nodded her head. "Well, I told him of our need, and God impressed him to donate a good lot worth $3,000. I'm sure some of the rent money from our old house will help to buy materials," Orley decided.

"And I know the new members will sacrifice to do all they can to build a little church," Lillian added.

By 1964, they felt they had established that church, so Orley told Lillian, "Let's go to another suburb in a different part of San Salvador. We have about a dozen members living there, but it's too expensive for them with their large families to travel by bus to the central church."

They worked hard, holding meetings in a little house set back in a banana grove. Again, God blessed their efforts. This new group, which they called Scandia, grew so rapidly that they knew they must find a bigger place to meet. But they had no money.

A young school teacher who had attended all the meetings came to Ford, saying, "I've told my mother all I've learned about Jesus, and she wants to see you. Would you visit her?"

"Of course. How can I find her?"

The girl hung her head, "She keeps a saloon where she sells *aguardiente*." Orley knew this to be a strong liquor which was far too popular with the people of El Salvador.

When Orley entered the rum shop, he saw a copy of the Law of God hanging on the wall. The mother seemed very happy to see him.

"I'm ashamed to come to your meetings because I'm a barmaid," she said. "But I believe everything my daughter has shared with me. Please help me buy a Bible and a song book. I plan to sell my shop and be baptized soon."

"Wonderful!" the pastor exclaimed. "You'll be so welcome in our new church, but, as yet, we have no place to build and no money with which to buy."

"That's another reason why I wanted you to come and see me." She smiled. "I own a lot worth at least $1,000 just a block from the big Catholic church. I want to donate it so you can build a church there. But if all my other children knew, except my daughter, they'd be very angry. Could we make out the papers right now so it will appear as a sale?"

Orley could hardly wait to get home. "Lillian, where are you?" he shouted from the front door. She hurried from the kitchen to meet him.

THE GREATEST OF THESE   69

"Jesus told us that the publicans, harlots, and, I might add, saloonkeepers will come in before those so-called better classes."

When he had told her what the Holy Spirit had done, she exclaimed, "Absolutely fantastic! God's 'something better' promises never cease to amaze me. This will be the third church God has helped us build since your retirement five years ago." Walking toward the dining room, she added, "Dinner's ready. Please come with me and meet more of our family. We now have four young girls from country churches living with us, and they will attend school across the street."

"Well, with you and the lady who helps you with the radio Bible school, plus our maid, that makes seven women to one man. That reminds me of Isaiah 4:1, where the prophet says that seven women shall take hold of one man," and Orley laughed.

The next Sabbath, the Fords accepted an invitation to visit a little mountain church. Usually only jeeps and trucks tried those almost impassable roads, but somehow Orley's little German Ford got through. They started at 5:00 a.m., drove fifty miles, left their car, and walked seven miles to where 200 people waited for them. How the people loved Lillian's melodica!

After Sabbath School and church, Orley pulled fifty bad teeth. Then he and Lillian walked another mile to a place where the pastor baptized five people.

"I hope we make it back to the car before that storm breaks," Lillian said, as she looked at the threatening sky. They made it just before the tropical downpour started.

"We'll have no trouble sleeping tonight," Orley commented, as they arrived home just before bedtime. "Especially with such a full day of visiting ahead of us."

Sunday morning, after breakfast, they went to the general hospital to visit a church member who had just had surgery. Next, they stopped at a home for the maimed, crippled, and aged. Not one of the 500 persons there had a normal body. Though many were senile or mentally deficient, a large number had alert minds but bodies deformed by arthritis or birth defects.

"Look, they've seen us." Lillian waved to a group seated in wheelchairs, obviously waiting for them. The Fords wheeled them out onto the patio under a large umbrella tree.

Orley smiled at the joy reflected in their faces as they sang choruses with Lillian and her accordion. How they listened to the Bible stories he told them! Already, Orley had carried seven of them into and out of the baptismal tank as they gave what was left of their lives to Jesus.

From there, they went to the home of a church member who couldn't come to church because of a bad heart and a terrible sore on her leg. Her husband spent most of his earnings on drink, so they had barely enough food.

There, in a shack not even eight-feet square, made of old boards, cartons, and tin cans, they found an old couple. The woman sat on the dirt floor before the fire preparing a scanty meal. When the Fords handed the man a sack of beans and rice, they noticed that his hand was badly swollen.

"Please come to our home, and I will give you some hot-and-cold water treatments. I know they'll help the infection," Lillian said. The Fords couldn't enter, for there was no room inside, so Orley prayed from the door.

Next they stopped at a little room where a mother held two small children, both crying.

"Are your babies sick?" Lillian asked.

"No, hungry. I'm out of work and have no money to buy milk."

Orley reached into his pocket. "Take this and buy what you need," he said.

Returning home, the Fords had just finished their midday meal when one of the girls rushed in. "Pastor Ford, an old man has fallen just outside our door."

Both of the Fords hurried out and recognized one of their oldest church members. Evidently he had come for help and had fainted because of weakness. They gave him first aid, but realized he was in serious condition.

"May we take you to the hospital?" they asked.

THE GREATEST OF THESE 71

"No, take me to my son's home. I'd rather die there," he whispered. Orley got out the Ford station wagon and gently took him to his son. After praying with him, Orley brought the old man his Bible and Sabbath School quarterly. The next morning they found him with a smile on his face, still clutching his precious books, awaiting the call of the Lifegiver.

The rest of that Sunday afternoon and evening, the Fords held their regular service at the jail. At their last visit to the tuberculosis sanitarium, they encouraged the twenty-five patients whom they had previously baptized. Weary from the long day, Lillian commented as they returned home, "How I long for Jesus to come, when He'll remove all misery, suffering, poverty, sickness, and pain."

All the while Ford continued to solicit money for the new church. Donations came only in dribbles due to the extreme poverty of the people. Orley had better success writing to friends back in the States. Realizing that the donated lot would be too small, he sold it and purchased a much larger lot in a more central location where new homes were being built.

"We must have room for a church school, too, Lillian. Only churches that provide for their youth will grow," Orley spoke with his usual foresight.

Construction began on the Scandia church in 1967. Orley did all the plumbing and carpentry work, even making the church benches. The congregation began worshiping in the building in July before they had even finished the construction.

A few weeks later came the big surprise! On July 22 the Fords celebrated two great events, their golden wedding anniversary and fifty years of mission service in Latin America.

"We're invited to the central church tonight, Lillian. Some type of special meeting," Orley said, with a twinkle in his eyes.

Nearly 1,000 people attended. Pastor and Mrs. Ford led a procession of all the workers and wives as they marched down the center aisle. When they took the honored seats on the platform, the master of ceremonies asked Lillian, "Have these fifty years seemed long to you?"

"Oh, no, they've been short, happy years full of thrills! True, I might have collapsed under some of the difficult times had I not had this fearless, strong young man by my side." Lillian smiled at Orley, then continued, "When we were surrounded by angry Indians, when sickness invaded our home and death took our three little ones, he was my refuge and source of courage. With him, I was not afraid."

"Other than in age, how have you changed from the young, inexperienced person who left your homeland for the mission field fifty years ago?"

"Only that God has blended the two of us until our desires, our ambitions, our likes and dislikes, have merged. We almost think alike. What has remained the same, both in times of danger and those of peace, is that we always find comfort kneeling together, committing our lives to our Father's care, and then lying down to sleep in confidence."

"And what are your plans for the future?"

"Our greatest desire is to keep our health so we can continue to work together for others until Jesus comes, and then go home with Him for all eternity."

After the service, the Fords found their home full of workers and friends who had planned a party for them. Many who had obtained an advanced education through the efforts and sacrifices of the Fords responded with gifts and special tributes of love and gratitude.

"How pleasant to be remembered with so many kind expressions of love," Lillian exclaimed after the guests had left.

When the Scandia church was going well, the Fords reached out to a suburb not too far away called San Roque. The few members living in that area joined with them in a series of meetings. Soon their numbers increased until they could no longer meet in homes. Again Pastor Ford helped them build their own little church building.

In 1969 Orley announced, "I think it's time we take a little vacation to the States."

"Good idea," agreed Lillian, "but first let's give ourselves a 'going-away present' by inviting the children from the *mesón* to our home for a party."

"Lillian, do you know what you're asking for?" Orley looked amazed. "Over 1,000 people must be crammed into that two-block slum area. Sometimes several families live together in just one small room."

"I know, Orley. I've been holding story hours with them for a long time. How I love to hear those dear little children sing! They're my friends, and I'd like to give them something special."

"Our big dining room might hold up to fifty people, but there must be hundreds of needy children living in the *mesón*," he objected.

"We'll have the party in the courtyard."

"I see you have it planned already, madam, so I might as well cooperate." Orley hugged his wife. "And what's for refreshments?"

"I think they'd like sandwiches, baked plantains (large orange-colored cooking bananas), and mangoes. I'll send each one home with a package of dried milk, plus some clothes from our Dorcas supply."

The Fords had a great time with the 215 children who came. When they left, the children called back to the gray-haired couple who waved from the gate.

"Have a nice holiday, but be sure you come back. You belong to us."

Chapter 13
Servants of the Lord

Orley Ford lived out his belief that a missionary must be able to do many things. He stated, "If he can't build his own house or repair his own automobile, he's destined to live in a shack and travel on foot."

Though Orley neared his seventy-ninth birthday and Lillian her seventy-eighth, having retired almost fourteen years before, they continued to work with the same youthful vigor. Pastor Ford explained:

"Our daily schedule varies with the demands. Still we have a set time for worship, meals, going to bed and getting up, and our afternoon siestas. Since visitors can depend on mealtime, they often drop in to enjoy Lillian's homemade bread and delicious, wholesome food, which she purchases each day at the local market."

No doubt their regularity and strict adherence to good health habits enabled the Fords to maintain the vitality necessary to help so many people. How else could they have conducted meetings, directed Pathfinder clubs, overseen the Dorcas Society, prepared and delivered many talks and sermons, and cared for all who asked for their hospitality? In addition, Orley showed weekly temperance films in schools, barracks, and business organizations. Continually, they enrolled students in the Voice of Prophecy Bible School, which Lillian directed.

Lillian showed her special interest in the children and youth, stating, "I love to plan hikes and mile walks, swimming parties at the beach, and nature games and activities that are fun. Everywhere I go, I carry my flannel board and felt figures to tell Bible stories to the children."

As a Pathfinder director, she excelled. Every year she and her helpers organized and planned a junior camp. No one thought it strange to see this gray-haired couple sleep in a tent, sing lustily around the campfire, and join in the nature honor classes and crafts. In addition, Lillian loved leading out and training others in conducting Vacation Bible Schools.

By 1972, Pastor and Mrs. Ford began to work with yet another group of believers in a suburb of the capital city called San Ramón. Orley thrilled at the rapidly growing number of people who gave their lives to Jesus when he made his calls each night at the meetings. With his usual drive and enthusiasm, he said, "I think it's time to begin thinking about a place to build another church."

The Fords believed in investing their funds in heaven's bank. Except for their living expenses, most of their retirement and Social Security checks helped to pay school expenses for Salvadoran youth or for the construction of these churches.

"I'm so glad for the financial blessing of our old house. The steady rent income has helped a lot," Orley told Lillian. "But now that I'm getting older and the house is constantly needing repair, I hope we can soon sell it."

About this time, Orley had an accident while driving in the precarious traffic of the city. His vision failed him on a street crossing, and another car crashed into the side of his German Ford. Though his injuries weren't serious, he needed time to recover.

"As usual, I'll snap back to normal in no time," he said.

But he didn't. Since healing came so slowly, he decided to get a checkup from the doctor. During the examination, they discovered that Orley had leukemia.

Then God, who knew Orley couldn't handle the repairs on his old house much longer, provided a buyer who gave him a good price for it. Included in the deal was a piece of land right beside the Villa Delgado church, which he had helped to build right after his retirement.

Elated, Pastor Ford exclaimed, "That little church has become far too small for their fast-growing congregation. Now they can build a new church and use the old one for children's rooms."

Then he added, "Psalm 46:1 is proving true again. How good of God to provide for our needs at just the right time. Now we can follow the doctor's recommendation and go to the U.S. for more modern treatment."

For six months, Orley had special care, but by the middle of September, his physician said, "Pastor Ford, the treatments are not arresting your disease. I fear you have only a few more weeks to live."

"Then I must get back to El Salvador and take care of some unfinished business. The little group at San Ramón does not yet have a place in which to meet. They need my help."

So Lillian and Orley returned once more to their beloved mission field. By this time he felt so weak, he had to lie down most of the time. But he did not suffer much pain. Hearing of his illness, many came to visit him.

"My life of service here is about over," he told them. "And I'm ready to meet my Lord. Now I want to be sure that you, too, have allowed Jesus to prepare you for that great day. Will you be reconverted again right now?" And the pastor prayed for each one.

On November 12, a visitor arrived that brought him both joy and relief. "Mr. Ford," he said, "I've come to finalize on the purchase of a very adequate building for the new church in San Ramón."

Orley's face, wreathed in smiles, glowed. "What a God! Again He is my refuge and strength, a very present help in time of trouble. He knows my time is running out, so He worked fast to supply a place for our new believers to worship Him. Now I feel that my work is done."

On Sabbath, November 18, the El Salvador Mission planned a special meeting called "The Day of Brotherly Love." Many came from all parts of the country. Everyone wanted Pastor Ford to be present.

"Mrs. Ford, would it be possible for us to carry him to the

afternoon meeting?" several of the brethren asked. "We have a cot on which he can rest."

"If he wants to go, I will not object. I know how he loves to be with his people. Go in and ask him."

"I'd love to be present," Orley said.

He enjoyed the fellowship of those for whom he had labored so long. Though he had very little strength, he asked for help to stand and give his last sermon to 2,500 of his beloved church members, speaking for about ten minutes.

"My dear friends, I'm sure this is the last time I shall meet with you on this earth," he said. "But what does it matter that I have only a short time here? All these years Jesus and I have walked and talked and worked together. Now my thoughts are on that blessed moment when I shall meet my precious Lord in the air.

"My concern is for you. Are you daily making the necessary preparation so that we can meet together when He comes to call His own? Some of us will rise from the grave, others will join us in the clouds. What a joyful reunion we'll have in the air! Oh, how glorious it will be to live forever with our Lord. We must all be there together. I shall be looking for each of you.

"My labors have ended. Be faithful, dear friends. Work enthusiastically. God will help you finish the work so we all can go home soon."

Exhausted, but with a deep sense of peace, Pastor Ford asked his brethren to help him back to the cot. Great joy showed on his face, as he lay listening to that huge congregation sing his favorite hymn,

> All the way my Saviour leads me;
> What have I to ask beside?
> Can I doubt His tender mercy,
> Who through life has been my guide?
> Heavenly peace, divinest comfort,
> Here by faith in Him to dwell;
> For I know whate'er befall me,
> Jesus doeth all things well.

That afternoon's exertion probably hastened his end. He felt so tired he could only drink the juice of three oranges. During the night, vomiting, diarrhea, and hiccups added to his weakness. Early the next morning they took him to the hospital. Lillian stayed by his side, as she had all those years. Holding her hand, he whispered, "You'll soon be alone now."

Two pastors, who stood beside her, said, "Let's pray." When they looked up from their prayers, Orley Ford had peacefully gone to sleep in Jesus at 12:45 p.m., on Sunday, November 19, 1972.

As a final tribute to their leader, the Pathfinders and Master Guides took their place among the flowers and wreaths as honor guards. They stood at attention beside the casket all night long and during the funeral, changing positions every half hour. When the ministers finished the service, church members prolonged this meeting of love by giving heartfelt tributes to their beloved leader, such as:

"To Pastor Ford, being a missionary was a lifelong dedication and commitment. He served happily, regardless of conditions, because he loved people."

"Though Pastor Ford never became proficient in speaking Spanish, we loved to hear him speak. His face always lit up with a glory from God we could see and understand."

"We cannot say that Pastor Ford was a great evangelist or a great administrator. His greatness lay in the fact that he loved the people, and thus they came to love God through him."

And how did Lillian cope? Though her heart was heavy with sadness, she went quietly about her duties, trusting Jesus for strength, comfort, and courage. She greeted all the callers, taking time to listen to each one. Yes, she greatly missed the man she had loved so much, but she kept on just as she had done before. Orley would have been proud to hear her say:

"I shall continue to live in the home that Orley built. With the help of the girls who are living with me, I can welcome all who come, whether it's for a day or a year. We can always find room for one more at the table, and usually a place to spend the night. I must keep the 'Ford Hotel' running. God will continue to give me good health, with my mind stayed on Him. God will help me bear my sorrow if I keep busy."

How did the young people of El Salvador accept a woman in her eighties? They loved her because she loved them. When they had a Pathfinder parade, who marched behind the drum and bugle corps in full uniform? The Pathfinder clubs with their helper and friend, Lillian Ford. Whom did the young people choose to be the one who pinned their Master Guide emblem on their neckerchiefs? They wanted Mrs. Ford, the one who had spent many hours enabling them to achieve this honor.

Lillian showed that she accepted reality in a remark she made at the Dorcas Society: "I'm sorry that my eyesight is not as good as it used to be. Now, instead of mending and sewing, maybe I'll do better at sorting clothes. I can still see the difference in sizes and quality. By the way," she added with a smile. "Do speak a little louder. I can't afford a hearing aid."

In the early 1980s, she experienced another blessing. Her son, Elden, and his wife, Venessa, stopped by to see her. "Mother, we have good news to share," Elden said. "I have just been asked to be the educational superintendent of the El Salvador Mission, with a special commission to establish a boarding academy. Won't you please come and live with us?"

"Wonderful! I'm so glad you'll be close to me. Orley would have been so pleased," she exclaimed. "Since our membership has grown to over 18,000 with so many youth of academy age, this is a great challenge.

"But," she hesitated, "I just don't feel I can close up our home here. I do appreciate your invitation so much, but who would serve the many people of this city who need a place where they know they're welcome?"

"As you wish, Mother, but I do feel this large home is getting too much for you to manage alone."

"I'm never alone," she objected. "I always have the Lord and the girls who stay with me, plus all the visitors that continually drop by."

"Well, we're only twenty-eight miles from the city." Elden

gave in. "If you change your mind, there'll be plenty of opportunity for you to serve there too. God has provided the money for the purchase of 228 acres of good, flat land suitable for agriculture, and the U.S Embassy has donated enough money to start building the Adventist Training School of El Salvador."

"And I can continue to give money to provide a Christian education for worthy students. With the academy only forty-five minutes away, I'm sure I can help when needed."

And so Lillian continued to serve the people she and Orley loved.

On the morning of October 10, 1986, this almost 92-year-old missionary awakened with a jolt. A terrible earthquake had struck El Salvador. Dishes, pots, and pans fell from the shelves. The water tank above the house cracked and poured water through the roof. Huge cracks appeared in the walls, but because of Orley's good construction they did not collapse.

As soon as he could, Elden came to the city to check on his mother. He found her, broom in hand, starting to clean up the rubble.

"Mother, this is too much for you. We'll hire some of the church members to do the job. The house needs extensive repairs. Please come home with us."

Wearily, she sank into a chair. "I've done a lot of thinking and praying this morning, son, and I think the time has come for me to rent this house and accept your invitation. Please help me pack up my things."

Just before they left the house, Lillian voiced her thoughts. "With every move, God always gave Orley and me something better. I must trust Him now until that glorious moment when I shall meet Jesus and Orley in the clouds and together we shall enjoy God's 'something better' for all eternity."